THE ORTON-GILLINGHAM EDUCATORS' GUIDE

FIRST EDITION

HEIDI BISHOP

DAVID KATZ

NORMA JEAN MCHUGH

LINCOLN TURNER

ABOUT THE AUTHORS

HEIDI BISHOP is a Fellow of the Academy of Orton-Gillingham Practitioners and Educators (AOGPE) and is a Certified Dyslexia Therapist certificate by the International Dyslexia Association (IDA). She has trained practitioners in schools and school districts thoughout SC, NC, GA, and CA. She served as president of the South Carolina Branch of the International Dyslexia Association for six years, was appointed to the SC Dyslexia Task Force, served on the Read to Succeed Advisory Group, and currently serves on the Information and Outreach Committee of the AOGPE board. She has spent 31 years working in private schools for children with dyslexia and is now involved with a dyslexic charter school that opens in the fall of 2018.

DAVID KATZ, a Fellow of the Academy of Orton-Gillingham Practitioners and Educators, has trained and mentored many practitioners in the Orton-Gillingham Approach. An experienced educator, David has a Master of Arts in Teaching degree and has taught at the elementary, middle, and high school levels. He also has extensive experience practitionering students through his private practice in Metuchen, New Jersey. David is active in the literacy community, serving as a past president of the New Jersey Branch of the International Dyslexia Association, an advisory board member of the New Jersey Learning Disabilities Association, and a lecturer at conferences throughout the United States and abroad.

NORMA JEAN MCHUGH is a Fellow and Board Member of the Academy of Orton-Gillingham Practitioners and Educators with over 30 years of experience working with dyslexic students. She initially worked at the Schenck School, a school for dyslexic students in Atlanta, Georgia. While at the school, she held many titles, including practitioner, creator of their summer camp for students, and director of their practitionering program. Upon leaving Schenck, she began training practitioners in the Orton-Gillingham Approach and has trained practitioners and parents. Norma Jean lives in Atlanta with her husband and enjoys spending time with her children and grandchildren.

LINCOLN TURNER is a lifelong educator and the co-founder of Whizzimo.com, the premier digital teaching platform for Orton-Gillingham based instruction. Lincoln received his Masters Degree in English Education from Columbia University's Teachers College and began his career in education as an English Teacher in the New York City public schools. Lincoln has trained and coached thousands of educators and school leaders throughout the United States on the best practices for literacy instruction.

A special thank you to Pat Golus for editing our guide

TABLE OF CONTENTS

Introduction to the Orton-Gillingham Approach 1

Who are Orton and Gillingham? 2

Overview of the Content in the Orton-Gillingham Approach 3

The Language Continuum 4

The Dyslexic Learner 4

Introduction to the Neurological Underpinnings of Dyslexia 6

The Red Flags of the Dyslexic Learner 11

Introduction to Language 12

Introduction to the Vowels and Consonants 12

How Vowel Sounds are Produced 12

The Third Vowel Sound: The Schwa (ə) 13

How Consonant Sounds are Produced 15

Phonological Awareness 16

Phonological Awareness Terms 16

The General Emergence of Phonological Awareness in the Child 18

The Hierarchy of Phonological Awareness 19

Basic Language Study Terminology 20

Concept of a Consonant 21

Consonant Digraphs 21

Consonant Blends 22

Concept of a Vowel 22

The Syllable 23

Introduction to the Six Syllable Types 24

Syllable Division Rules 28

Conclusion to the Syllable 34

Spelling Rules and Spelling Generalizations 34

Ending Spelling Rules 36

Spelling Rules for Plural Nouns 40

Multiple Spellings 43

Spelling Generalizations 44

Exceptions for Closed Syllable 45

Silent Letter Combinations (ghost letters) 45

Non-phonetic Words/Red Words/Sight Words 46

Introduction to Morphology 50

Prefixes and Suffixes 51

Prefixes: Numbers 52

Prefixes: Position 53

Suffix List 53

The Three Sounds of –ed 53

Roots: Verbs 55

Roots: Nouns/Describing Words 56

Words of Origin 56

The Diagnostic and Prescriptive Elements of Orton-Gillingham 58

Introduction to the Concept of Scope and Sequence 58

Sample Scope and Sequence 59

Introduction to The Multisensory Elements of the Orton-Gillingham Lesson 66

Visual-Auditory-Kinesthetic-Tactile 66

Integration of Handwriting 67

Introduction to Fluency, or Blending, of Sounds 68

Error Correction 69

The Orton-Gillingham Lesson Plan 71

The Warm-Up 72

The Drill Pack 72

The Visual Drill 72

The Auditory Drill 73

The Blending Drill 74

Review and Reinforcement 74

New Information 76

Oral Reading.. 77

Keeping the Lesson Diagnostic and Prescriptive.. 78

The Student Notebook.. 79

Understanding the Needs of the Individual Student 82

The Student Profile.. 82

Medical History 83

Family History 83

Educational History 83

Testing Information 83

Previous Orton-Gillingham Instruction 84

Informal and Formal Instruments 84

Informal Assessments 87

Formal Assessments 90

Examples of Assessment Tools 92

Going Beyond Phonemic Awareness and Phonics: Grammar, Comprehension, and
Writing.. 93

Building the Sentence 95

The Paragraph and Expository Text.. 96

Signal Words... 98

Writing 99

The Big Five Paragraph/The Basic Paragraph 100

The Big Five Essay/The Five Paragraph Essay 101

Comprehending and Writing Narrative Text (Fiction) 105

Four Important Aspects of Comprehension 105

Integrating Reading and Writing 107

The Orton-Gillingham Classroom 109

Bulletin Board #1: Letters Are Talking! 111

Bulletin Board #2: Six Syllable Families 114

Bulletin Board #3: Let's Divide! 117

Bulletin Board #4: Affixes Help You Understand! 121

Bulletin Board #5: Follow the Rules! 124

Bulletin Board #6: Sentences Need… 128

Bulletin Board #7: Paragraphs Need 130

Bulletin Board #8: Read to Learn 132

Additional Resources 134

Wordlists 135

VC Words 135

CVC Words A-Z 135

Digraphs 136

Consonant Blends 137

Syllable Types 139

Syllable Division Types 142

Organization of a Student Binder 143

Developmental Tasks for Phonological Awareness 144

Sample Orton-Gillingham Lesson Plan #1 145

Sample Orton-Gillingham Lesson Plan #2 149

Sample Orton-Gillingham Lesson Plan #3 152

Sample Scope and Sequence #1 154

Sample Scope and Sequence #2 155

Check Off List for the Auditory Drill 156

Letters Checklist 158

Orton-Gillingham Checklist 160

    Consonants 160

    Consonant Digraphs.. 160

    Vowels 160

    Vowel Teams - Diphthongs.. 161

    Syllable Types 161

    Spelling Rules 161

    Spelling Generalizations 162

    Other Patterns 162

    Syllabication Rules... 162

Reading Vowel Chart... 163

Reading Chart for Consonant Letters... 165

Rule Chart.. 167

Six Syllable Types Chart... 168

Spelling Categories.. 169

Spelling Chart #1 170

Spelling Chart #2 172

Vowel Teams... 173

Ways to Divide Words into Syllables.. 174

Orton-Gillingham Approach – Three Strands 175

Manner of Articulation.. 176

Additional Handouts... 177

INTRODUCTION TO THE ORTON-GILLINGHAM APPROACH

Making the Student an Active Reader!

Orton-Gillingham is an approach to teaching the structure of language. It is based on years of study about the brain and how we learn, combined with the logical, sequential building blocks of language. Each lesson is prescriptive, diagnostic, and individualized. This means that each lesson is based on the needs of the individual. Lessons always begin with the most basic components of language and move as quickly or as slowly as students' needs dictate.

Dr. Orton's Language Triangle

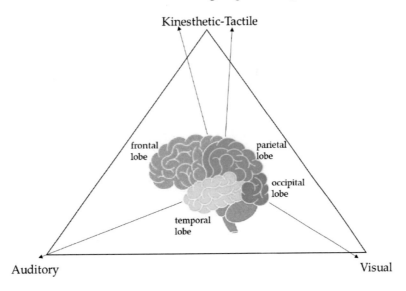

Orton-Gillingham is not a rigid program that only works for some students and leaves educators without the necessary knowledge to individualize instruction. Rather, it is an approach that uses multisensory techniques for learning. All of the senses are engaged simultaneously in order to create the neural network that students need to manipulate the components of language structure. The Orton-Gillingham approach is also multisensory because it engages the visual (eyes), auditory (ears), kinesthetic (muscles), and tactile (fingers/touch) pathways in the learning process.

1

The idea of multisensory learning is that students must be actively engaged in the process of reading, so they can become more proficient.

Educators should understand how the brain works. It is also helpful to have a background in the history and structure of language, an understanding of the Alphabetic Principle, and a knowledge of the difference between vowels and consonants.

Instruction should build logically from small to large, simple to complex, and known to new.

WHO ARE ORTON AND GILLINGHAM?

Samuel T. Orton was a neurologist and psychiatrist who is referred to as the "father of dyslexia." Orton was the first to identify the syndrome of developmental reading disability and to offer a physiological explanation for its cause. In 1925, Dr. Orton, Chairman of the Department of Psychiatry at the University of Iowa College of Medicine, conducted a study of 14 children with severe reading delays. He wanted to know why these children, all with average to above average IQ scores, were unable to read. Dr. Orton theorized that reading problems in these individuals were due to the inability of the left hemisphere to become dominant over the right. Orton coined the term, strephosymbolia, meaning "twisted symbols," to define why dyslexics' brains are unable to establish appropriate cerebral organization that would enable them to associate the visual and auditory components. Dr. Orton's revolutionary insight brought the concept of multisensory instruction (visual–auditory–kinesthetic/tactile) into the classroom.

Anna Gillingham was a psychologist and director of remedial teaching. She, and educator Bessie Stillman, took the research of Orton, integrated phonics, and published *The Gillingham Manual* (Educators Publishing Service) in 1936, with later editions in 1946, 1956, and 1960. Gillingham and Stillman spent years creating and developing a sequential, multi-sensory approach to teaching language. They realized that alphabetic phonics, where sounds and letters are taught and used to construct words, was the key to helping all children gain the ability to read. As a result, they developed a way to teach instructors how language develops from the simple to the more complex concepts that make up our ability to communicate.

OVERVIEW OF THE CONTENT IN THE ORTON-GILLINGHAM APPROACH

Orton-Gillingham covers all the components of language development, from sound/symbol awareness to reading comprehension and essay writing. The following list provides the topics covered in the Orton-Gillingham approach:

- The Sounds of Language
    - How speech is produced
    - The difference between vowels and consonants
    - Voiced and unvoiced speech sounds
    - The segmentation and manipulation of sounds
    - The rhythm, stress, and intonation of speech
- Sound/Symbol Associations
- Separating Sounds and Syllables for Reading (Decoding)
- Combining Sounds to Enable the Spelling of Words (Encoding)
- The Six Syllable Types
- Syllable Division Rules
- Spelling Rules and Generalizations
- Morphology
    - The structure and meaning of words
    - Roots, prefixes, and suffixes
    - The use of semantics and syntax
- Grammar
    - The classification of words
    - Combining words to form sentences
    - The types of sentences
    - The rules of punctuation and capitalization

- Combining Sentences to Form Paragraphs
- Comprehension and Written Expression
  - The types of paragraphs
  - Combining paragraphs to form essays and compositions
  - The types of compositions
  - The types of texts
  - Outlining structures
  - The elements of symbolic and figurative language

THE LANGUAGE CONTINUUM

Listening, Speaking, Decoding (Reading), Encoding (Spelling), Fluency, Comprehension, and Writing.

The language continuum looks at the use of language from the sound/symbol association to the ability to communicate with others. Everyone has strengths and weaknesses in the use of language. Some have proficiency in reading comprehension while having great difficulty reading with fluency. Others have strong fluency skills but are unable to put thoughts on paper. Still others have no difficulty reading and writing but find it challenging to retrieve words when speaking. All of these elements come together as we interact with text and each other.

THE DYSLEXIC LEARNER

The word dyslexia is derived from the Greek *dys* (poor or inadequate) and *lexis* (words or language).

According to the Academy of Orton-Gillingham Practitioners and Educators, dyslexia can be summarized as "difficulty in the use and processing of arbitrary linguistic / symbolic codes. This is an aspect of a language continuum, which includes spoken language, written language, and language comprehension" (February 1995).

According to the International Dyslexia Association and the National Institute of Child Health and Human Development, "Dyslexia is a specific learning disability that is neurobiological in origin. It is characterized by difficulties with accurate and/or fluent word recognition and by poor spelling and decoding abilities. These difficulties

4

typically result from a deficit in the phonological component of language that is often unexpected in relation to other cognitive abilities and the provision of effective classroom instruction. Secondary consequences may include problems in reading comprehension and reduced reading experience that can impede growth of vocabulary and background knowledge" (November 2002).

Characteristics of Dyslexia include:

- Lack of awareness of sounds in words, rhymes, or the sequence of sounds and syllables in words
- Difficulty decoding words (word identification)
- Difficulty encoding words (spelling)
- Poor sequencing of numbers and letters in words, when read or written
- Difficulty expressing thoughts in written form
- Delayed spoken speech
- Imprecise or incomplete interpretation of oral language
- Difficulty expressing thoughts orally
- Problems with reading comprehension
- Confusion about directions in space or time
- Confusion about right or left handedness
- Difficulty with handwriting

INTRODUCTION TO THE NEUROLOGICAL UNDERPINNINGS OF DYSLEXIA

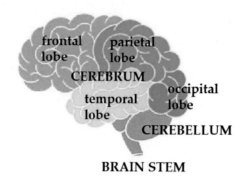

REVIEW OF THE BRAIN AND THE CENTRAL NERVOUS SYSTEM

The Nervous System is comprised of a constantly developing system of cells that are created and evolve in biological preset stages, beginning at conception and continuing into adulthood. The basic unit of the nervous system is the nerve cell or neuron. There are many forms of neurons, but all have a cell body, axon, and dendrites. Electrical or nerve impulses received by the dendrites pass through the cell body and down the axon, where they are picked up by other dendrites. The nerve impulses are conducted from one nerve cell to another across a space called the synapse, through the actions of chemicals called neurotransmitters.

The human brain weighs about three pounds and has four main components: the cerebrum, the diencephalon, the brainstem, and the cerebellum. For our studies, we will look primarily at the cerebrum and the cerebellum.

The cerebrum is the largest area of the brain. It is made up of two hemispheres joined together by nerve fibers called the corpus callosum. This area serves as a communication pathway between the hemispheres. Both hemispheres are divided into four lobes (frontal, temporal, parietal, and the occipital).

In a fetus, the cerebral surface appears smooth. As the complexity of the brain increases, indentations gradually appear. By late childhood, the surface of the cerebrum has become very convoluted with many furrows and humps. These forms are like storage areas for the brain. In the dyslexic person, fewer convolutions have been noted. In a low functioning individual, even less of these convolutions are evident. (Galaburda)

The left hemisphere is considered the language control center of the brain (Orton 1937, Geschwind 1968). Expressive language is controlled in the left frontal lobe in Broca's area, named after Dr. Paul Broca. Dr. Broca realized how this area of the brain was important for the organization, production, and manipulation of language and speech after studying a stroke victim (Joseph, Noble, & Eden, 2001).

Receptive language is centered in Wernicke's area, located in the left temporal lobe. This region was identified by Carl Wernicke who found that language is understood and processed in this location.

The ability to link spoken and written language to memory and to understand what we hear and read takes place in the parietal lobe.

The primary visual cortex is important for the identification of letters. This is located in the occipital lobe.

The cerebellum is the part of the brain that controls movement and coordination. It has been called the "brain's main timing device" (Stein, 2001).

NEUROLOGICAL FINDINGS

Reading depends on the quality of the brain's processing of visual and auditory input. It requires a highly sensitive magnocellular system. This entails that the magnocellular neuron is able to function, while the left and right hemispheres of the brain can adequately communicate (Stein and Walsh 1997, Demonet 1993). Recent MRIs have shown that reading involves both hemispheres of the brain, but the importance of the left is enhanced as phonological demands are made, while the right side is more important for detecting rhythms and intonation of speech.

Recent studies have found that certain areas of the brain are indeed formed differently in the dyslexic reader. It is now clear that the cerebellum, which controls the timing of information and which receives dense inputs from all magnocellular systems, is deficient in dyslexics (Fawcett 1996, Rae 1998, Nicolson 1999). The findings show that reduced sequencing and timing of dyslexics may be due to impaired function of the cerebellum as information moves from the right hemisphere to the left hemisphere.

Researchers have begun to conclude that the limitations of the cerebellum manifest as incomplete automatization of information. Discussions and studies of the dyslexic student often turn to the double deficits of speed and phonology as positive indicators of dyslexia. Therefore, the dyslexic student has difficulty developing automatized skills.

As researchers Angela Fawcett and Roderick Nicolson explain. "Consequently, if one wishes to minimize the literacy problems of children with dyslexia, it is necessary to give specialized teaching designed to automatize the subskills involved through carefully designed, carefully monitored, and long-term training programs. This is directly consistent with established good practice guidelines for supporting children with dyslexia, which stress that an exceptionally structured, explicit, systematic and comprehensive approach is needed, progressing in small steps, with each step mastered before the next one is introduced" (Gillingham and Stillman 1960).

Researchers have also noted evidence that static cerebellar signs, such as poor postural stability and muscle tone, may distinguish children with dyslexia as well. Other studies have found that dyslexics show differences in cell size and cell size distribution in the posterior and anterior cerebellar cortex (Nicolson and Fawcett 2001). These researchers call for the "re-introduction of learning as the central theme in studies of learning disability."

Many of the researchers have studied the connection between the cerebellum and the two hemispheres of the cerebrum. Rapid Automatized Naming (RAN) testing has been used from studies in the 1970s (Denckla and Rudel) to the more recent work of Wolf and Bowers in 1999. These tests have tried to determine how rapidly children can retrieve phonetic information. Think of this as students' anticipatory processing abilities. A variety of tests have been introduced, and researchers point to the importance of early screenings, starting at kindergarten. RANs are usually made up of cards with rows of pictures of familiar objects, which children must name as quickly as they can.

This testing is certainly not perfect. However, data has consistently shown the link between visual and auditory processing. When individual letters and sounds are not processed in close temporal proximity, it impedes the formation of the orthographic patterns linked to phonological representations (Wolf 1992).

Ultimately, researchers have continually come to the conclusion that RAN testing must be conducted with tests that can assess the child's knowledge and control of letter names/letter sounds and phonological awareness. As reported by Berniger in 1995 and Badien in 1997, "impaired readers suffer from three deficits: phonological awareness, naming speed, and orthographic awareness, and that all three processes can have effects on reading."

This same idea was discussed by researcher Maryanne Wolf (2000), who said that an approach to reading intervention will require, at minimum, the use of a) naming speed measures (RAN) to aid the early identification of students struggling for a double deficit in reading (phonological procession deficit and a naming speech deficit), and b) interventions that focus strategically on the development of fluency and automaticity in the component skills of reading.

One recent study to examine Wolf's contentions came up with similar conclusions (Keme'enui 2001). This study of 328 kindergarten students compared three interventions designed explicitly to promote the development of foundational skills in beginning readers. A pre-test/post-test comparison group design with the random assignment of subjects to groups was used to examine the effects of various types of instruction on the reading development of kindergarten students identified as struggling for reading difficulties. The study compared the Phonological Awareness Spelling (PAS), Phonological Awareness Storybook (PASB), and the Sounds and Letters and Story Thinking from Open Court (OC) assessments. The results found that the most successful program was PAS, which provided students with explicit, systematically designed instruction of phonological awareness and alphabetic understanding.

Recent studies using the type of testing discussed above have been conducted with MRIs. Repeatedly, research has indicated the lack of neural firing in the left hemisphere of the cerebrum. Also noted was a difference in the neural firing between the right and left hemispheres.

Brain images taken of dyslexic children before they received structured spelling instruction clearly showed the lack of neural firing, leading to poor automaticity. However, after intensive work with structured spelling instruction, the MRIs showed brain activity with patterns that more closely followed that of the proficient speller (2006).

Researchers have also begun to study the relationship between dyslexia and attention deficit hyperactivity disorder (ADHD). At this point in time, the complete nature and extent of this association is not understood, but patterns have become evident between the two disorders. Researchers now believe that, "There are numerous points at which attentional functions intersect with the process of reading. The process of reading involves a complex combination of phonological analysis and visual/attentional functioning with integrated ocular movements. Because effective reading is heavily dependent on attentional and intentional factors, it is not hard to understand why many children with dyslexia also have some degree of attentional dysfunction" (Voeller 1999).

CONCLUSIONS

Recent use of MRIs has brought much new knowledge and understanding to the neurobiology of dyslexia. However, researchers agree that much more is still to be discovered about dyslexia and the central nervous system.

Findings continue to show a kind of failure of the "left hemisphere rear brain system" to function during reading and writing.

Studies continue to show that explicit, intense, systematic instruction in the sound structure of language (phonemic awareness) and in how sounds relate to letters (phonics) benefits the dyslexic learner.

Studies also show that students with a better understanding of dyslexia and their individual learning style develop a healthier self-image and are better motivated to succeed academically.

THE RED FLAGS OF THE DYSLEXIC LEARNER

Children who have dyslexia often first exhibit signs of a language deficit with the inability to develop oral language as quickly as their peers. Therefore, the first educational intervention is in the area of speech remediation. However, when looking at the development of speech, it is quite evident that having weak language skills is not just the inability of the child to have clear articulation. Oral language competency is the ability of the child to initiate language, ask and answer questions in complete sentences, and understand directions. The dyslexic child who suffers from weak speech skills will often have difficulty in the beginning of sound/symbol associations that lead to reading fluency. Delayed speech can lead to organizational problems in the eventual activities of reading comprehension and written expression.

Ultimately, the deficits in the use of language are not just a reading or writing issue. Dyslexia encompasses the entire language continuum because all elements of language, which embody oral and written language, come together as we interact with each other.

INTRODUCTION TO LANGUAGE

Language can be defined as the process by which meanings are exchanged between individuals through a system of sounds and symbols.

Music, mathematics, Morse Code, sign language, and English are all man-made languages. These systems of symbols developed overtime and became commonplace because people agreed to recognize and communicate with them.

While human beings are born with brains that are "wired" for speech, they must be explicitly taught how to read and spell.

The sounds that vowels and consonants make are called phonemes. There are over forty phonemes, and they can be differentiated by their acoustic properties, the way they are produced by the vocal chords, and their function in blending speech sounds into intelligible words. Phonics is the system of associating these speech sounds with letter symbols using phonetics, the science of speech.

INTRODUCTION TO THE VOWELS AND CONSONANTS

The English language is based on the Alphabetic Principle, where letter shapes represent sounds and those sounds are blended into syllables and words. There are two types of sounds - vowels and consonants. They differ in two important ways: 1) how the sounds are produced, and 2) how the sounds are used.

HOW VOWEL SOUNDS ARE PRODUCED

Vowel sounds are produced by an unobstructed flow of air.

All vowel sounds are called "voiced" sounds because the vocal chords vibrate when they are used. The mouth must be open to make a vowel sound. The sound is not obstructed by the speech organs: the lips, tongue, and teeth. In fact, vowel sounds can go on for as long as the person has breath. The vowel sounds are the "bridge" between the consonants. Without the vowel sounds, we would not be able to communicate with each other.

For example, the letters *bttrfl* cannot be pronounced until the vowels are added, and the word *butterfly* is created.

Therefore, every syllable must have a vowel sound. The important fact to remember is that a vowel can have several different sounds when pronounced. Most often, the sound of a vowel is either long or short.

In the dictionary, the symbol for a long vowel sound is the macron - which means "long" in Greek. It is a straight line placed right above the vowel.

$$/\bar{a}/ \ /\bar{e}/ \ /\bar{\imath}/ \ /\bar{o}/ \ /\bar{u}/$$

The symbol for a short vowel sound is the breve, which means "short" in Latin. It is shaped like the bottom part of a circle.

$$/\breve{a}/ \ /\breve{e}/ \ /\breve{\imath}/ \ /\breve{o}/ \ /\breve{u}/$$

THE THIRD VOWEL SOUND: THE SCHWA (ə)

Many multisyllabic words have a middle syllable that is unstressed and has a neutral sound called the SCHWA. In the dictionary, it is shown as *ə*.

This happens because the syllable in front of the open syllable is being stressed.
Think of the schwa as if you are taking a breath of air. It sounds like "uh."

$$\overset{\text{ə}}{}$$

daffodil   daf/ fo/dil

In the dictionary, the word daffodil is followed by the actual pronunciation of the word enclosed in parentheses. Here, you can see the schwa symbol: daf´ ə dil´.

You will notice that the first and third syllable have an accent mark above them. This denotes that these syllables are being stressed. The middle syllable, which is the schwa, is unstressed and has the schwa symbol.

That is why many words are difficult to pronounce and spell. Younger students may not understand the concept of the schwa, but students in 3rd grade and up should be introduced to the concept of schwa and the unstressed versus stressed syllables. This will assist them in developing their reading fluency.

WHAT DOES SCHWA SOUND LIKE?

It is difficult to hear the difference between a short /u/ sound and the schwa /uh/ sound. Here are some points which may help you. The schwa sound is very similar to the short /ŭ/ sound, but it is softer, or weaker. The schwa phonics sound is the /uh/ sound of a vowel in an unstressed syllable.

Here are some words which will help you hear the schwa phonics sound. Schwa says the short /uh/ sound in:

- the first vowel sound in /about/
- the last sound in /the/

INTERESTING FACTS ABOUT THE SCHWA SOUND!

- It is the only phoneme with its own name.
- It is the most common vowel sound in spoken English.
- It is often referred to as the third sound of the single vowel sounds.
- It is represented by the linguistic upside-down e symbol ə.
- All vowels can be used to spell the schwa sound.
- The schwa word comes from an ancient Hebrew word which means "emptiness or no vowel sound."

This is considered a "neutral" sound. It is also referred as a "mid central" vowel sound that is unstressed. The sound is /uh/ and all five vowels can be used as the spelling of this sound. This is one reason spelling can be so difficult. The schwa occurs as a sound in spoken English, but the only time you would see the schwa symbol ə is in the dictionary when it is used as a pronunciation symbol.

Example: alone /ə lōn/

The schwa is a crucial component of the auditory element. Many words are mispronounced when the schwa is forgotten or unknown to the students. This is especially true in multisyllabic words. Since the schwa is unstressed in a syllable, the alternating syllable has an accented or stressed sound.

Examples (with schwa sound underlined):

pi l<u>o</u>t   pres <u>i</u> dent   un <u>o</u>b struct ed   en cy cl<u>o</u> pe di a

Therefore, every educator should be aware that there are three vowel sounds when they are introducing the elements of reading:

1) long
2) short
3) schwa

One quick note with respect to locating the accented syllable in a word. A trick is to act like you are calling a dog in from the outside. For example, when calling a dog named "Sparky," you will naturally accent the first syllable. This is true for most other words. Simply pretend the word is a dog that you are calling, and you will be able to identify the accented syllable.

HOW CONSONANT SOUNDS ARE PRODUCED

Consonant sounds are produced when the flow of air is obstructed.

This happens because the speech organs (including the teeth, tongue, and the back of the throat) obstruct the flow of air. Most consonant sounds are "unvoiced," meaning the vocal cords do not vibrate.

When introducing the vowels and consonants to students, you can incorporate the concept of voiced and unvoiced speech sounds. One crucial component of this is helping the students understand how their body produces the speech sounds. The practitioner can have the students place two fingers on their throat as they say the phonograms aloud. They will feel their vocal chords vibrate when pronouncing the voiced sounds.

PHONOLOGICAL AWARENESS

Simply put, phonological awareness is the awareness that there are sounds in our language that make up spoken words. This refers to syllables, parts of syllables, and individual sounds.

Phonological awareness is important to have because children who lack phonological awareness skills will have difficulty learning the relationship between letters and the sounds they represent. They will also have difficulty applying the letter/sound correspondences that allow them to "sound out" unknown words.

Thankfully, phonological awareness can be developed through practice. The following sections will define the types of activities that can be used to develop phonological awareness, as well as providample questions for each activity type.

PHONOLOGICAL AWARENESS TERMS

Listed below are definitions of some important phonological awareness terms. Each definition is followed by a sample question for the instructor and sample tasks that students may complete when assessing or practicing that specific skill.

Rhyming is the ability to identify or produce words that rhyme.

Type	Task
Discrimination	Do *mat* and *cat* rhyme? How about *map* and *mop*?
Production	Tell me a word that rhymes with *bit*.

__Matching__ is the ability to identify identical sounds.

Type	Task
Phonemes	Tell me a word that ends with the same sound as the word *friend*.
Syllables	Do *jumping* and *thinking* begin with the same syllable?

__Counting__ is the ability to identify the number of sounds in a word.

Type	Task
Phonemes	How many sounds are in the word *shrink*?
Syllables	How many syllables are in the word *everlasting*?

__Segmentation__ is the ability to hear individual sounds or sound units.

Type	Task
Phonemes	Can you say each sound in the word *mop*? /m/ /o/ /p/
Syllables	Can you clap for each part of the word *Atlanta*? At-lan-ta

__Deletion__ is the ability to manipulate spoken words by removing specific sounds.

Type	Task
Phonemes	Say *tan*. Now say it again but don't say the /t/.
Compound Words/Syllables	Say *blackboard*. Now say it again without the *black*.

__Substitution__ is the ability to manipulate words by substituting certain sounds for others.

Type	Task
Initial	Say *pat*. Change the /p/ to /h/ - hat.
Final	Say *man*. Change the /n/ to /t/ - mat.
Medial	Say *look*. Change /oo/ to /i/ - lick.

Blending is the ability to say a word when provided with the individual phonemes.

Type	Task
Phonemes	I'll say the sounds of a word and you guess what the word is. /r/ /i/ /g/ = rig /p/ /a/ /t/ = pat
Compound Words / Syllables	I'll say the parts of the word and you guess what the word is. *bun-ny*

Isolation is the ability to identify the first, middle, and/or last sounds in a word.

Type	Task
Initial	Tell me the first sound in the word *tree*.
Final	Tell me the last sound in *truck*.
Medial	Tell me the middle sound in the word *mat*.

THE GENERAL EMERGENCE OF PHONOLOGICAL AWARENESS IN THE CHILD

It is usually between the ages of one to eighteen months when a child begins to understand that the sounds he is making have meaning. The child is now able to use a word even when a certain object is not in front of him. This is the beginning of true speech.

Around eighteen months or so, the child comes to understand simple directions and begins to put two words together. Now the child is building his vocabulary to about 20-25 words.

Usually, by the age of two and a half, the child can name 4–5 objects, speak in simple phrases, and has a growing vocabulary of 200+ words.

By the age of three, children usually can speak in simple sentences with pronouns and comparatives. The vocabulary may have grown to about 900 words.

At the age of four, it is common for children to be able to name all types of common objects encountered in everyday life. They are able to name colors and shapes, as well as name animals and tell the sounds animals make. At this point, ta child has a vocabulary of about 1,500 words.

By the age of five, children use descriptive words and can compare and contrast in their sentences. They can count to ten. All speech sounds should now be present and intelligible. Children should be able to blend sounds to form words, and then break sounds up to hear the individual phonemes (sounds). They should come to understand how words can rhyme.

THE HIERARCHY OF PHONOLOGICAL AWARENESS

Another way to look at the development of phonological awareness is to look at a timeline for the development of specific tasks for children who are not experiencing any learning challenges.

- Preparatory Activities
  - o Develop listening habits – Preschool-Early Kindergarten
  - o Tune into print - Preschool-Early Kindergarten
- Rhyme Awareness Activities
  - o Identify words that rhyme - Preschool-Kindergarten
  - o Produce words that rhyme - Preschool-Kindergarten
- Phoneme Awareness Activities
  - o Identify the beginning sound of a word - Preschool-Kindergarten
  - o Identify the ending sound of a word - Preschool-Kindergarten
  - o Identify the middle sound of a word – Kindergarten-First Grade
- Segmenting Activities
  - o Segments sentences into words - Preschool-Kindergarten
  - o Segment words into syllables - Preschool-Kindergarten
  - o Segment words into sounds – Kindergarten-First Grade
- Blending Activities
  - o Blend syllables into words – Kindergarten-First Grade
  - o Blend sounds into words – Kindergarten-First Grade
- Manipulation Activities
  - o Delete syllables from words – First Grade
  - o Substitute syllables in words – First Grade
  - o Delete sounds from words – First Grade

o Substitute sounds in words – First Grade

A Sample Phonological Activity Incorporating Many Elements of the Heirarchy

airplane

How many syllables? <u>**2**</u>
How many sounds in the first syllable? <u>**2**</u>
How many sounds in the second syllable? <u>**4**</u>
If you take off the first syllable, what is left over? <u>***plane***</u>
*Change **plane** to **port** and what is your new word?* <u>***airport***</u>

BASIC LANGUAGE STUDY TERMINOLOGY

The following terms are central to the study of language. We will discuss them in more detail in subsequent sections.

- **Language** – a rule-based system of symbols (spoken, written, ideas).
- **Grapheme** – a single letter or letter combination that represents a phoneme.
- **Phoneme** – the smallest unit of speech that serves to distinguish one utterance from another.
- **Phonics** – the system of associating letter symbols with speech sounds.
- **Phonetics** – the scientific study of speech sounds.

- **Phonology** – the study of the sound system of language.
- **Morphology** – the study of how morphemes (the smallest unit of meaning) are joined together to form words.
- **Morpheme** – the smallest meaningful unit of language.
- **Free Morphemes** – words that can stand alone.
- **Bound Morphemes** – parts of words in conjunction with a root word.

CONCEPT OF A CONSONANT

Things to know about the consonants:

- There are 21 consonants: (b c d f g h k l m n p q r s t v w x y z)
- Consonants rarely say their names (like *x* in x-ray)
- Most consonants have 1 primary sound
- The letter *r* does not say *er*. It sounds more like a barking dog - /r/
- The letter *q* is followed by *u* in all English words.
- No word in the English language ends in *v* or *j*.
- *v* is always followed by *e* at the end of a word (e.g. love, give, active).
- Consonants are either voiced or unvoiced.

Voiced Sounds	Unvoiced Sounds
d (dog)	**t** (top)
v (van)	**f** (first)
b (boy)	**p** (pan)
z (zebra)	**s** (sink)
g (go)	**k** (kite)
j (jump)	**ch** (chin)
th (that)	**th** (thin)

CONSONANT DIGRAPHS

Although each consonant makes a sound, there are also two- and three- letter consonant combinations that also make only one sound. These groups of two and three consonants are called consonant digraphs.

The most common consonant digraphs are *ch, sh, th, wh, ck, tch* and *dge*. Some of these digraphs, like *wh*, only occur at the beginning of the word while others, like *tch*, only occur at the end of a word.

CONSONANT BLENDS

While a consonant digraph consists of two or three consonants that make one sound, a consonant blend consists of two or three letter consonant combinations that make more than one sound.

The most common type of consonant blend consists of two or three consonants, each of which makes its own sound. For example, *sl* (slow), *st* (fast), and *spl* (split) are all consonant blends.

Another type of consonant blend consists of a consonant digraph plus a single consonant. Examples of this type of consonant blends are *shr* (shrink), *chr* (chrome), and *thr* (three).

Three-letter consonant blends are often also referred to as *consonant clusters*.

CONCEPT OF A VOWEL

Things to know about vowels:

- All single vowels have more than one sound; they all make a long sound, a short sound, or a schwa sound.
- 60% of English words have short vowel sounds.
- A single vowel followed by a consonant is usually short (*at, bog, did, cat, bat, plot, plug*)
- A vowel followed by the following letters is usually not short: *r, l, w, y.* (e.g. *curb, call, cow, delay*)

THE SYLLABLE

Letters become syllables and syllables become words…

Using the example *bttfl* and *jllfsh,* adding vowels to the consonants yields *butterfly* and *jellyfish,* two words that are recognizable.

This example shows that each syllable must contain a vowel sound in order for us to be able to pronounce it.

A syllable is:

- One push of the breath.
- It has one vowel sound.
- That sound can be long, short, or schwa.
- There are six syllable types.

Try this:

Place one hand directly in front of your mouth and say the word *purr.* You should feel a slight push of breath on your hand as you exhale. Now say the word *propel,* and notice that you feel two pushes of breath on your hand as you exhale twice. Each is a syllable.

Here is another example that shows how each additional syllable in a word adds another push of breath. Say these words in order:

- *re*
- *respect*
- *respective*

There is a difference between a *vowel* and a *vowel sound*. For example, the suffix *-ed* has the vowel *e*, but it doesn't always make a vowel sound. Here are a few two-syllable words where *-ed* has a vowel sound:

- lift**ed**
- mend**ed**

And here are some two syllable words where *-ed* does not have a vowel sound:

- film*ed* (the *-ed* makes the /d/ sound.)
- help*ed* (the *-ed* makes the /t/ sound.)

INTRODUCTION TO THE SIX SYLLABLE TYPES

The six types of syllables are listed below using the common acronym *CLOVER*.

<u>C</u> = <u>C</u>losed
<u>L</u> = Consonant-<u>l</u>e
<u>O</u> = <u>O</u>pen
<u>V</u> = <u>V</u>owel Team (vowel digraph, vowel diphthong, vowel pair)
<u>E</u> = Magic-<u>E</u> (Silent e)
<u>R</u> = <u>R</u>-Controlled (r-combination, vowel-r, bossy-r)

Please note that while *CLOVER* is a helpful acronym, the syllable types are not typically introduced in this order. ĕ

CLOSED SYLLABLE

The closed syllable is typically the first syllable studied because many of the simplest and most common words are one-syllable words.

The easiest way to understand a closed syllable is that it has a single vowel that is "closed" in by one or more consonants after the vowel.

For example, the word *cat* has one single vowel, and the letter *a*, is "closed in" by the letter *t*.

Another characteristic of the closed syllable is that the vowel sound is usually a short vowel sound unless it is a part of a two or more syllable word. For example, the *e* in web says /ĕ/; the *e* in happen has a schwa sound /ə/.

The simplest types of closed syllable words are called *VC* and *CVC* words. *VC* words consist of a single short vowel followed by a single consonant, as in words like *in, at,*

24

ox, and *up*. **CVC** words consist of a single consonant, followed by a single short vowel, followed by a single consonant, as in the words like *win, tax, fox, cup*. Once a student has a solid understanding of **VC** and **CVC** words, they can begin creating longer closed syllables by adding consonant digraphs and blends.

For example, a logical progression might be *at -> cat -> chat -> chant.*

Another type of easy-to-decode multisyllabic word is compound words that contain two or more closed syllables. Compound words will be covered in the section on syllable division, but compound words are simply words that are comprised of two words that can stand alone. Examples of compound words that consist entirely of closed syllables are *sunset* (sun/set) and *cobweb* (sun/set).

Key takeaway - a closed syllable is two to seven letters long and has a single vowel which is typically short because is followed by one or more consonants.

OPEN SYLLABLE

While a closed syllable is "closed" because a single vowel is followed by one or more consonants, an open syllable is "open" because a single vowel is located at the end of a syllable, as in words like *hi* and *go*. As the previous examples show, when the syllable is open, the vowel typically makes the long vowel sound.

The simplest type of open syllable follows the **CV** pattern – a single consonant followed by a single vowel. Examples include *ba* as in *ba*sin, *no* as in *no*tate, and *ra* as in *ra*cer.

Similarly, there are open syllable words that have initial consonant digraphs and blends followed by one vowel. Examples include *cra* as in *cra*dle, *tri* as in *tri*pod, and *the* as in *the*sis.

Open syllables become more common when we start studying multisyllabic words.

Another common type of open syllable includes the y /ē/ at the end of multisyllabic words. One type of open syllable containing *y* occurs when *y* is part of a suffix in words like *windy* and *quickly*. The letter *y* also occurs at the end of words, as in *baby* and *lady*.

In words like *windy* and *quickly*, the syllable types are easily combined in multisyllabic words. Both of those examples contained a closed syllable followed by an open syllable. **Key takeaway** – open syllables end with a single vowel that typically makes the long vowel sound.

MAGIC-E/SILENT-E SYLLABLE

Magic-e syllables, also commonly called Silent-e syllables, are identified by the following pattern: *Vowel+Consonant+e* (or *VCe*). In the word *ate*, the vowel *a* is followed by the consonant *t* and the silent letter *e*. This is the *VCe* pattern.

So why is this syllable type referred to as "magic"? It is more of a teaching strategy than anything else because practitioners often tell students that the letter *e* has a "magical power" that allows it to be silent but makes the vowel (like the letter *a* in *ate*) say its name.

Once the *VCe* pattern is recognized, it can be seen in larger one-syllable words like *cake* (*CVCe*) and *state* (*CCVCe*). The *VCe* pattern is even present in one-syllable words with suffixes on the end like names and plac*ed*.

Magic-e syllables are also present in multisylabllic words such as *likely* and *useful*.

Key Takeaway – Magic-e syllables (also called Silent-e syllables) have the *Vowel+Consonant+e* pattern where the *e* is silent and the vowel sound is long.

R-CONTROLLED SYLLABLE

R-Controlled syllables earn their name because the letter *r* controls the vowel sound in the syllable. For example, the word *car* may appear to be a closed syllable, but it is nearly impossible to pronounce with a short *a* sound. When the word *car* is pronounced normally, the letter *r* alters and controls the sound of the letter *a*. (This is probably why R-Controlled syllables are sometimes also referred to as *Bossy-R* syllables.)

The most common R-Controlled syllables contain *ar* (c*ar*), *er* (h*er*), *ir* (f*ir*), *or* (n*or*), and *ur* (f*ur*). These are the first legger combinations taught, but *yr* can also create R-Controlled syllables as in words like s*yr*up. As with the other syllable types, digraphs (Mar<u>ch</u>), blends (<u>fl</u>i*r*t), and suffixes (pa*rk*<u>s</u>) at the beginning and ending of R-Controlled syllables can be added to create longer one-syllable words.

There are several other types of R-Controlled syllables.

Another type of R-Controlled syllables has two r's pronounced as a single r sound. Examples of these types of words are c*urr*ent, s*orr*y, m*irr*or, b*err*y, and c*arr*ot.

R-Controlled syllables can also consist of two vowel letters followed by *r*. Examples include *oar* (b*oar*), *air* (h*air*), and *eer* (pion*eer*).

The letter *w* before *ar* and *or* can alter the vowel sound, as in the words *wor*th and *war*m.

Key takeaway – An R-Controlled syllable has at least one vowel followed by an *r*. The vowel sound is neither long nor short. The *r* controls the vowel sound.

VOWEL TEAM SYLLABLE

The word *boat* has two vowels, but there is only one vowel sound because the vowels have "teamed up" to make the long o sound. This is a vowel team - vowel letter combinations that combine to make up a syllable's vowel sound.

There are over 25 vowel teams. Among the most common are *ai, ay, ee, oa* and *ie*. These vowel teams are often introduced first because they have long, pure, vowel sounds.

The characteristic of diphthongs, a type of vowel team, is that the mouth changes position as it produces the sound. The *oi* in c*oi*n is a good example of a diphthong.

The letter *w* can be a part of a vowel team in the following letter combinations: *aw* (s*aw*), *ew* (gr*ew*, f*ew*), *iew* (view), and *ow* (snow, cow).

Key takeaway – vowel team syllables contain vowel letter combinations that make a single sound.

CONSONANT-LE SYLLABLE

Consonant-le syllables are the only syllable type without a sounded vowel that is only found at the end of a multisyllabic word. For this reason, consonant-le syllables are easy to locate. As the name suggests, a consonant-le syllable contains a consonant followed by the letters *l* and *e*. The *e* is always silent, so the consonant and the *l* usually form the syllable's sound. For example, in the word *simple, ple* is a consonant-le syllable, and the syllable's sound is /pul/. For this simplest type of syllable, the syllable begins three letters from the end of the word ("count back 3").

Key takeaway – consonant-le syllables occur at the end of multisyllabic words and contain a *consonant + l + e*.

SYLLABLE DIVISION RULES

As students are learning and reviewing the six syllable types, they begin to recognize them in the multisyllabic words they are asked to read. The next step is learning how to divide these words into syllables. This is something that fluent readers do automatically, but it is a skill that needs to be taught to emerging readers.

The syllable rules that we will cover below are:
- One-Syllable Words
- Compound Words
- Prefixes, Roots, and Suffixes
- Consonant-le
- The VCCV Pattern
- The VCCCV Pattern
- The VCV Pattern
- The VV Pattern
- A Vowel can be a Syllable by Itself

Accurate syllable division is important because it is essential to proper pronunciation and, therefore, to comprehension.

Fluency is the ability to smoothly and accurately blend the phoneme sounds into syllables and words at an even and steady pace. Identifying the six syllable types, knowing the vowel sound in each syllable, and recognizing where syllables end and begin is an essential step in the progression of fluency.

The goal is for students to look at a word, find the vowels, and look for the pattern.

RULES FOR DIVIDING WORDS INTO SYLLABLES

ONE-SYLLABLE WORDS

A one-syllable word is never divided.

Every syllable has only one vowel sound. This sound can be short, long, or schwa. Even if a syllable has more than one vowel letter, it can only have one vowel sound. This knowledge helps students look for the vowels in syllables to determine what kinds of syllables they are sounding out.

Beginning students will only be learning about a closed syllable pattern called the *CVC* pattern. The other five syllable types can be introduced as each previous syllable is understood.

Examples of *CVC* words include *cat* and *nip*.

COMPOUND WORDS

A compound word is divided between the two words of which it is comprised.

The introduction of the compound word provides a great opportunity for the integration of the syllable types.

Many students can recognize the words within compound words because they may be words they have seen before. For example, it is not surprising that younger children have an easier time recognizing words like *birthday* and *playtime* because they contain words that gain their attention. Reading drills using compound words offer a way to review the syllable types while developing comprehension.

However, compound words introduced to students can only be made up of syllable types that have been previously introduced. If the student has only been introduced to *CVC* words, then the compound words must only include words with the closed syllable type like **catnap** (cat/nap) and **sunset** (sun/set).

As additional syllable types are introduced, compound words can now feature these syllables.

THE *VCCV* PATTERN

When two consonants come between two vowels in a word, syllable division is usually between the consonants, *VC/CV*. This pattern is often the second pattern presented to a student because words are mostly made up of CVC, closed syllables.

This pattern is more challenging to recognize because the separate syllables may only convey meaning when they are joined together: rec/kon.

In order for the students to gain fluency reading this word pattern, they must look for the vowels in the word and find the pattern: *VCCV*. Also, if the two consonants being divided are the same letter, the students might call them "twins." We call these the *rabbit* words.

	vc cv		vc cv
rabbit =	rab/bit	picnic =	pic/nic

In the *VCCV* pattern, the first syllable will often be closed and have a short vowel sound.

At this time, if students are ready to be introduced to the concept of the open syllable with a long vowel sound, they can read words that end in the vowel *y*. Students will learn that at the end of multisyllabic words, the vowel *y* has the long sound of vowel *e*, and that this syllable is open.

vc cv

sunny = sun/ny

THE *VCCCV* PATTERN

When students are reading multisyllabic words which contain consonant blends and digraphs, they can be introduced to the *VCCCV* pattern.

Students still "look" for the vowels and "find" the pattern, but they must divide the word into syllables, while not separating the blends and digraphs.

vc ccv   vc ccv

monster = m<u>o</u>n/st<u>e</u>r   panther = p<u>a</u>n/th<u>e</u>r

Sometimes there are more than three consonants between the vowel, as in words like **instruct** and **diphthong**. It is important to break the word up keeping appropriate blends, clusters, and digraphs together (in/struct; diph/thong).

THE *VCV* PATTERN

 These next two dividing rules may be the most important for the students to learn:

V /CV   and   VC/V

These two patterns clearly demonstrate that dividing a word at the wrong place, yields an incorrect vowel sound; hence, a misread word. Remember that vowel sounds can be long or short. Vowels are short when they are in a closed syllable and a consonant is at the end.

When looking at a multisyllabic word with a *VCV* pattern, the students must decide if they should divide the word before or after the consonant. In most words, the correct place for division is before the consonant:

v cv

hotel = h<u>o</u>/t<u>e</u>l

The first syllable is open and the vowel sound is long.

However, if students divide a word before the consonant and the word does not make sense, then they should divide the word AFTER the consonant.

$$\underline{V}/CV \qquad\qquad \underline{VC}/\underline{V}$$
$$r\bar{o}/b\underline{i}n \quad \text{when it should be} \quad r\breve{o}b/in$$

The key is for the students to "find" the vowels, "look" for the pattern, and decide where to divide the word.

Words that fit the **V/CV** pattern are often referred to as "tiger" words (tī/ger), and words that fit the **VC/V** pattern are often referred to as "camel" words (căm/el).

V/CV	or	VC/V
se/ven	or	sev/en
rad/ar	or	ra/dar
hot/el	or	ho/tel
e /lect	or	el /ect
riv/er	or	ri/ver

CONSONANT-LE

When a word ends in *le* preceded by a consonant, the word is divided before that consonant.

As discussed in the section on the six syllable types, this syllable is unique because it is found only at the end of a multisyllabic word, and it does not have a vowel sound. The consonant-le syllable is also an important aspect of syllable division. In most cases there are three letters in this syllable and the suggestion is to count out the three letters - *consonant, l, e* or *1, 2, 3*. However, this syllable can also have 4 letters with combinations like *ckle* and *stle* and when adding the suffixes *-s* or *-ed*.

candle	=	can-*dle*
table	=	ta-*ble*
needle	=	nee-*dle*
marble	=	mar-*ble*
chuckle	=	chu*ckle*
whistle	=	whi*stle*
bubbles	=	bub-*bles*
tickled	=	tic-*kled*

THE *VV* PATTERN

When two vowels come together in a word and are sounded separately, divide between the vowels: *V/V*

This pattern can be difficult for students to find because the vowels look like a vowel team.

<u>V</u> <u>V</u>   <u>V</u> <u>V</u>   <u>V</u> <u>V</u>   <u>V</u> <u>V</u>

diet = di<u>/e</u>t   violin = vi<u>/o</u>/lin   lion = li<u>/on</u>   poet = p<u>o/e</u>t

A VOWEL CAN BE A SYLLABLE BY ITSELF

When a vowel is sounded alone in a word, it forms a syllable by itself. */V/*

monument = mon/u/ment   disobey = dis/o/bey

Usually, the separate vowel has a long sound because the syllable is open.

PREFIXES, ROOTS, AND SUFFIXES

A word is divided between an affix (prefix or suffix) and a root word.

The introduction of the Latin and Greek roots and affixes should be a part of language instruction starting in kindergarten. The classical roots are introduced as content is presented in a subject area: language arts, social studies, science, and math. Each root is a syllable which has other syllables called prefixes and suffixes attached to it in order to convey meaning. In Latin, *affix* means *to fasten on*, and that is exactly what the student is learning to do. Ultimately, students learn that word parts do not stand alone. They come to realize that prefixes, roots, and suffixes carry information that can help them understand the meaning of new words. For example, when young children are learning the word *triangle*, even if they cannot actually read the word, they can learn that *tri* means three.

Morphology, the study of word meaning, should be integrated into all content curriculum. For example, a few of the words that can be created that include the root word *ject* (to throw):

reject	project	deject
rejecting	projecting	dejecting
rejected	projected	dejected

CONCLUSION TO THE SYLLABLE

To help students blend syllables together, remind them:

- Letters become syllables, syllables become words
- Every syllable must have a vowel sound
- Vowel sounds can be short, long, or schwa
- In vowel team syllables, there is only one vowel sound
- In magic-e/silent-e syllables, *e* is silent; there is only one vowel sound
- Look for the vowels in a multisyllabic word and listen to the sounds (see chart below).
- Figure out where one syllable ends and the next syllable begins.
- Remember the types of syllables and the rules for dividing words into syllables (look for the number of vowels and the number of vowel sounds heard).

Chart

Word	See	Hear		# of Syllables
pencil	2	2	=	2
jeep	2	1	=	1
basement	3	2	=	2
peanuts	3	2	=	2
wagon	2	2	=	2
supermarket	4	4	=	4
sailboat	4	2	=	2

SPELLING RULES AND SPELLING GENERALIZATIONS

Knowing spelling rules can assist students in reading fluency, reading comprehension, writing, and spelling.

The ability to encode (spell) and decode (read) words is enhanced when students have gained a proficient connection between sound/symbol associations of phonograms, the six syllable types, and the rules of syllable division.

Better decoding skills enable students to develop smooth and accurate blending of phoneme sounds into syllables and words at an even and steady pace, or fluency.

Students begin to realize that knowing the six syllable types, syllable division rules, and spelling rules can help them more quickly recognize words when reading.

Spelling patterns are consistent most of the time and spelling rules assist students as they encounter new vocabulary in the content areas.

The following spelling rules and generalizations will be covered:

- Ending Spelling Rules
    - THE F.L.S. (Floss) Rule - also called the FLSZ Rule
    - The *k/ck* Spelling Generalization
    - The *ch/tch* Spelling Generalization
    - The *ge/dge* Spelling Generalization
    - The Doubling (1-1-1 and a vowel) Rule
    - The Drop the e (Silent-e) Rule
    - The Y to I Rule
    - The 2-1-1 Doubling Rule
- Spelling Rules for Plural Nouns
    - Plural Nouns: -s or -es?
    - f to v Plural Rule
    - Plural Rule
    - Irregular Plural Rules
- Possessive Rules
    - Singular Possessive Rule
    - Plural Possessive Rule
- Multiple Spellings
- Spelling Generalizations
    - Soft c and g

- o   Hard c and g
- Closed Syllable Exceptions
  - o   all, alk, and alt
  - o   'Most Kind Old Wild Colt' Words
- Silent Letter Combinations (ghost letters)
- Non-phonetic Words/Red Words/Sight Words
  - o   The Red Words/The Rule Breakers

ENDING SPELLING RULES

These rules aid students in seeing how suffixes can change the form and meaning of words.

THE F.L.S. (FLOSS) RULE - ALSO CALLED THE FLSZ RULE

 f, l, s, and *z* are usually doubled at the end of one-syllable words directly after a single, short vowel.

staff	smell	kiss	buzz

This spelling rule is usually the first one to be introduced. When students are learning about the closed syllable and short vowel sounds, this is an excellent opportunity to present how spelling rules can help reading and spelling.

Students need to be aware that there are exceptions to each spelling rule. It is not necessary to have them memorize the exceptions to each rule, but they can learn them when necessary.

The following are exceptions to the FLS Rule:

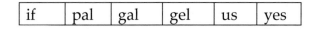

if	pal	gal	gel	us	yes

THE *K/CK* SPELLING GENERALIZATION

ck is used to spell the /k/ sound at the end of one-syllable words directly after a single, short vowel.

păck	nĕck	quĭck	blŏck	clŭck

ck is also used to spell the /k/ sound directly after one, short vowel in multisyllabic words when it is followed by *-et* or *-er*.

jacket	bucket	racket	cracker	rocker

Use *k* to spell the /k/ sound after a consonant or a vowel team.

bank	peek	link	speak

Use *ke* to spell the /k/ sound after a long vowel sound.

bāke	līke	spōke	Lūke

THE *CH/TCH* SPELLING GENERALIZATION

tch is used to spell the /ch/ sound at the end of one-syllable words directly after a single, short vowel.

pătch	strĕtch	hĭtch	blŏtch	crŭtch

Suffixes can be added to words ending in *-tch*.

pitcher	catching	kitchen	stretched

Use *ch* to spell the /ch/ sound after a consonant.

branch	starch	pinch	belch

Exceptions (think of **WØRMS**):

Which	**Ø**	**R**ich	**M**uch	**S**uch	

THE *GE/DGE* SPELLING GENERALIZATION

dge is used to spell the /j/ sound at the end of one-syllable words directly after a single, short vowel.

| bădge | lĕdge | brĭdge | lŏdge | fŭdge |

ge says /j/ after a consonant, a long-vowel sound, or after two vowels.

Consonant after the vowel	Long vowel sound	Two vowels
barge	cage	scrooge
fringe	page	beige
range, strange, change*	rage	

* Contains a long vowel sound and a consonant following the vowel.

THE DOUBLING (1-1-1) RULE

When a one-syllable word has one, short vowel followed by one consonant (the last three letters ending in a CVC), double the final consonant is doubled before a suffix beginning with a vowel. If the suffix begins with a consonant, no doubling occurs.

mad	+	est	=	maddest
mad	+	er	=	madder
mad	+	ly	=	madly

THE DROP THE E (SILENT-E) RULE

When a word ends in a silent *e*, the *e* is dropped when adding a suffix that begins with a vowel.

use	+	ing	=	using
use	+	d	=	used

When a word ends in silent *e*, the *e* remains when adding a suffix that begins with a consonant.

| use | + | ful | = | useful |

hope	+	ful	=	hopeful
safe	+	ly	=	safely

The magic-e/silent-e syllable keeps the vowel sound long when the suffix is added.

Exceptions:

- Final *e* is kept to make *c* or *g* soft (/s/ /j/) when adding *-able* or *-ous*:

trace	+	able	=	tra*ce*able
change	+	able	=	chan*ge*able
courage	+	ous	=	coura*ge*ous

- In the following words, the *e* is dropped:

wholly	awful	duly	argument	ninth

- The following words can be spelled with or without the *e*:

judgment/judgement	acknowledgment/acknowledgement	abridgment/abridgement

These rules are important for reading fluency and spelling:

- Is the bunny *hoping* or *hopping*?
- Is it time for *dinner* or *diner*?
- Was he *tapping* or *taping* on the front door?
- Will we go horseback *riding* or *ridding*?
- Is he *mopping* or *moping* the floor?

THE Y TO I RULE

When a word ends in a consonant directly before *y*, change the *y* to *i* and add the suffix.

cry	+	es	=	cr*i*es
cry	+	ed	=	cr*i*ed

Do not change the *y* to *i* before the suffix *ing* as in **crying**

If the *y* is part of a vowel team, then the *y* must stay.

| play | plays | playing | played |

Students need to be reminded that when adding *-s*, with or without a spelling change, the original word moves from a singular noun to a plural noun.

Singular	Plural
story	stories
pony	ponies

Singular	Plural
boy	boys
key	keys
tray	trays

THE 2-1-1 DOUBLING RULE

When adding a vowel suffix to a base word that has two or more syllables, the final letter of the base word is doubled if the accent is on the base word's final syllable.

be gin'	+	ing	=	beginning
com mit'	+	ed	=	committed

SPELLING RULES FOR PLURAL NOUNS

PLURAL NOUNS: -S OR -ES?

Plural nouns are words that mean more two or more. By the time children are in first grade, the passages that are read will include the plural forms of words in order to tell a story. Learning about *-s* or *-es* at the end of a root or base word aids in the development of fluency, reading comprehension, and spelling.

When a noun ends in *ch*, *sh*, *s*, *ss*, *x*, or *z*, add *-es* to the end to form to plural. Most other nouns are changed to the plural by adding *-s*.

Teaching this rule should start with words that only need to add the letter *-s*.

cat ⇨ cats	shirt ⇨ shirts	book ⇨ books

When the digraphs *sh* and *ch* are introduced, as well as *x* and words that end in *ss* and *zz*, students are ready to learn about forming plurals using *-es* at the end of the word.

brush ⇨ brushes	rich ⇨ riches	box ⇨ boxes
buzz ⇨ buzzes	glass ⇨ glasses	floss ⇨ flosses

F TO V PLURAL RULE

When a noun ends in *f* or *fe,* its plural is made by changing the *f* or *fe* to *ve* and *s*.

lea*f* ⇨ lea*ve*s	wol*f* ⇨ wol*ve*s	wi*fe* ⇨ wi*ve*s	thie*f* ⇨ thie*ve*s

The following words can be spelled both ways:

dwarf	dwarfs or dwarves
scarf	scarfs or scarves
hoof	hoofs or hooves
wharf	wharfs or wharves

O PLURAL RULE

When a noun ends in *o*, the plural is formed by adding *s*.

radio	=	radios
video	=	videos
hippo	=	hippos
photo	=	photos

However, some nouns ending in *o*, the plural is formed by adding *-es*.

The most common of these nouns are:

hero	=	heroes
veto	=	vetoes
potato	=	potatoes
tomato	=	tomatoes

IRREGULAR PLURAL RULES

Some plural nouns are irregular plurals and are spelled without adding *-s* or *-es*.

Singular		Plural
child	=	children
foot	=	feet
woman	=	women
mouse	=	mice

Some plural nouns have the same spelling as the singular form.

deer	fish	fruit	moose	sheep
swine	trout	Chinese	Japanese	species

Possessive Rules

SINGULAR POSSESSIVE RULE

Singular possessive nouns are formed by adding *'s* to the singular form of the noun.

owl*'s* eyes
pig*'s* tail
child*'s* backpack
house*'s* window

Singular possessive pronouns do not have an apostrophe.

mine	my	your	yours	his	hers	its

PLURAL POSSESSIVE RULE

If a noun is plural possessive (ends in an *-s* or *-es*), an apostrophe (') is added to make it possessive

cars	cars' tires
foxes	foxes' den
heroes	heroes' welcome

42

knives	knives' handles

If the plural is irregular, add *'s*:

men	men's
swine	swine's
geese	geese's

MULTIPLE SPELLINGS

Because there is more than one way to spell a long vowel sound, vowel teams and consonants can have more than one sound.

Students should have a list of multiple spellings in their notebooks, and a list should also be placed on a bulletin board in the classroom.

Below is a list of multiple spellings that highlight long vowel sounds. The sections are divided to separate the more commonly used spellings, the ones usually introduced first, and the less common spellings below the space. These are usually taught after the common spellings.

Long ā	Long ē	Long ī
a in an open syllable	*e* in an open syllable	*i* in an open syllable
a-e in a magic e syllable	*e-e* in a magic e syllable	*i-e* in a magic e syllable
ai as in rain	*ee* as in need	*igh* as in igh
ay as in day	*ea* as in meat	*y* as in sky
	y as in candy	
eigh as in eight	*ie* as in piece	*ie* as in pie
ei as in vein	*ei* as in ceiling	*y-e* as in type
ey as in they	*ey* as in key	
ea as in steak		

Long o	Long u	
o in an open syllable	*u* in an open syllable	
o-e in a magic e syllable	*u-e* in a magic e syllable	
oa as in coat		

ow as in snow	
oe as in toe	ue as in statue
	ew as in stew
	eu as in feud

Phrases and sentences that help students remember the multiple spellings for long vowel sounds are:

_a_ l_a_t_e_ r_ai_ny d_ay_ (long a)

Sh_e_ and St_e_v_e_ n_ee_d to _ea_t cand_y_. (long e)

_I_ l_i_k_e_ the n_igh_t sk_y_. (long i)

J_o_ will h_o_p_e_ for a c_oa_t for sn_ow_. (long o)

h_u_mid J_u_n_e_ (long u)

SPELLING GENERALIZATIONS

A spelling generalization is possible to predict because it happens frequently.

SOFT C AND G

The letter _c_ says /s/ and _g_ says /j/ when followed by _e_, _i_, or _y_. When this happens, _c_ and _g_ are said to make a "soft" sound.

ce	ci	cy	ge	gi	gy
cent	city	cycle	general	giant	gym
cell	cite	cyst	German	ginger	
center	circle	Cyprus	gentle	giraffe	

Some are exceptions to this rule are:

girl	get	give	gift

HARD C AND G

The letter *c* says /k/ and *g* says /g/ when followed by *a*, *o*, and *u* and consonants. When this happens, *c* and *g* are said to make a "hard" sound.

ca	co	cu	ga	go	gu
can	control	cut	gas	got	guy
case	court	current	garden	good	guess
came	common	culture	game	going	guard

EXCEPTIONS FOR CLOSED SYLLABLE

Most closed syllable words have short vowel sounds. However, there are some exceptions to this rule. The most common exceptions to the traditional closed syllable sounds are *all, alk, alt, ost, ind, old, ild, olt, oll,* and *olk*.

ALL, ALK, AND ALT

The letter *a* says /aw/ when the letter combinations *all, alk,* and *alt* are present.

all	alk	alt
small	walk	salt
ball	chalk	alter
install	talking	waltz

'MOST KIND OLD WILD COLT' WORDS

o says /oh/ when the letter combinations *ost, ind, old ild, olt, oll,* and *olk* are present.

ost	ind	old	ild	olt	oll	olk
most	find	hold	child	colt	roll	yolk
host	mind	fold	wild	bolt	troll	folk

SILENT LETTER COMBINATIONS (GHOST LETTERS)

Sometimes only one of the letters of a combination is heard. Silent letter combinations are comprised of 2-3 letters where only one of the letters is heard. Because they are seen and not heard, silent letters are sometimes called ghost letters.

At one time, each of these silent letters were pronounced, but they became silent after spelling became standardized.

Sometimes in multisyllabic words, silent letters are pronounced like **_signature_** and **_bombardier_**.

Common silent letter combinations that make consonant sounds are:

wr /r/	wring
kn /n/	know
mb /m/	lamb
rh /r/	rhythm
gn /n/	gnat
gh /g/	ghost
mn /m/	column

NON-PHONETIC WORDS/RED WORDS/SIGHT WORDS

The overwhelming majority of English words are phonetic. This means that they can be read and spelled based on the rules of our language. However, there are English words that are non-phonetic, meaning they can only be read and spelled from memory. For example, the word **_was_** cannot be sounded out; it must be memorized.

Below are two lists of non-phonetic words, including sublists of words that should be taught together. These words should be taught gradually over time, with the instructor keeping track of the words that have been learned and the words that have yet to be learned.

THE RED WORDS/THE RULE BREAKERS

As students read passages, they begin to notice that some words do not sound correct or they seem to be spelled incorrectly. These are the non-phonetic words, usually referred to as **_sight words_** or **_red words_**.

There are sight words that are so commonly used, that new readers will see them as they read even the most basic sentence:

The cat *is doing* a jump *off the* bed.

In this sentence, the words *the, is, doing,* and *off* are *red words* because they are not sounded the way they are spelled. These words must be memorized over time. The practitioner will introduce these words as needed. Because they cannot be pronounced, these words are not used in spelling drills.

Nonphonetic Rote Memory Word List A

a	are	could	door
again	bear	do	friend
against	been	does	from
always	both	done	give
any	come	don't	goes

gone	one	sure	want
guess	only	talk	was
guest	other	tear	wear
guide	pear	the	were
guy	people	their	what

have	pretty	there	would
hour	pull	they	you
live	push	though	your
love	put	through	youth
much	rich	to	

nothing	said	too
of	says	toward
off	should	two
often	son	very
once	such	walk

47

Groups to Be Taught Together

once	could	to	bear
one	should	too	pear
only	would	two	tear
			wear

who	such	you
whom	much	your
whose	rich	youth
	which	

Nonphonetic Rote Memory Word List B:

among	build	clothes	enough
another	built	cough	eye
blood	busy	debt	flood
break	buy	double	floor
broad	calf	doubt	four

fourth	listen	sew	trouble
front	many	soft	truth
gauge	month	some	usual
great	move	steak	Wednesday
group	muscle	straight	whole

guard	ninth	sugar	wolf
half	ocean	swore	won
heart	pint	sworn	wore
hearth	prove	thorough	worn
height	rough	tough	

honest
honor

iron			
island			
laugh			

Groups to Be Taught Together

great	rough	guard	heart
break	tough	guess	hearth
steak	enough	guest	
		guide	calf
		guy	half

blood	hour	group
flood	honest	soup
	honor	

wore	double
worn	trouble
swore	
sworn	

INTRODUCTION TO MORPHOLOGY

As students continue to practice and have become proficient integrating the six syllable types into multisyllabic words, the concept of prefixes, suffixes, and Latin and Greek Roots, as well as the parts of speech can be introduced. Students must now come to understand how morphemes also provide meaning.

Students can be shown that prefixes, suffixes, and roots carry information that can help them to understand the meaning of new words. This is crucial in the comprehension of content area curricula: science, social studies, math, and literature.

A *morpheme* is the smallest unit of meaning in language. A *free morpheme* can stand alone where a *bound morpheme* must be connected to another morpheme.

Free Morpheme	Bound Morpheme	Word
friend	*un-* *-ly*	*un*friend*ly*

Affixes refine meaning and can change a part of speech.

Prefix (Refines Meaning)	Baseword	Suffix (Changes the Part of Speech)	Word
dis-	honest	*-ly* (adjective – adverb)	*dis*honest*ly*

Prefixes are often open or closed syllables with a pure long vowel sound or a short vowel sound and are found before a free or bound morpheme. These types of prefixes are the most common, and students are using the affixes to see how meanings change.

tie	*un*tie	*re*tie
pack	*un*pack	*re*pack

Suffixes can change the meaning of a word and are found after a free or bound morpheme. Depending on the age and grade level of the students, suffixes help to teach the concepts of tense, along with the descriptive use of adjectives and adverbs.

For example:

walk	walk*ing*	walk*ed*
hope	hope*ful*	hope*less*
deep	deep*er*	deep*est*
care	care*ful*	care*fully*
child	child*ish*	child*ishly*
accept	accept*able*	accept*ably*

Root words are best introduced to students when they can assist them in the comprehension of curriculum content. For example, in a social studies class, if the students are learning about the *exports* and *imports* of goods from one country to another country, the root *port* (to carry) can be introduced.

The students can then use prefixes to better understand the meaning of moving goods from one country to another country:

ex = out   *port* = to carry   *export* = to carry or send out

im = into   *port* = to carry   *import* = to carry or bring in

Prefixes and suffixes are easier to read than roots because they are usually open and closed syllables with either a long or short vowel sound. Latin and Greek affixes and roots are easier to read with fluency than some simple, one-syllable words.

PREFIXES AND SUFFIXES

Examples of prefixes that are found in open syllables:

re = again
de = down, apart
pro = forward
pre = before

When added before a magic e/silent-e syllable, two syllable words with only long vowel sounds are created.

remake, restate, relate, rebate, retake, revoke, remote, revise,
debate, decline, decode, define, demote, decrease
provide, provoke, promote, profile,
predate, precede,

Some suffixes are easy to sound out and come right after a long vowel sound.

Some suffixes are considered stable, final syllables because they are often found in the final syllable and do not change pronunciation or spelling.

tion	sion	cial	cious	ture
motion	fusion	racial	spacious	future
ration	confusion	crucial	gracious	nature
lotion	conclusion	glacial	voracious	
potion	inclusion	facial	ferocious	
station	erosion	social		
nation	occasion			
vacation				

Students begin to see how affixes give meaning to new words. The knowledge of spelling rules can assist them in recognizing words more quickly when reading, and fluency is developed. Furthermore, students can see how words change meaning when sentences are read.

Below are lists of common prefixes, suffixes, and roots:

PREFIXES: NUMBERS

Prefix	Meaning	Example
mono-	one	monopoly
uni-		unicorn
bi-	two	bicycle
du-		duet
tri-	three	triangle
quad-	four	quadrangle

oct-	eight	**oct**opus
dec-	ten	**dec**ade
cent-	hundred	**cent**ury
milli	thousand	**milli**on

PREFIXES: POSITION

Prefix	Meaning	Example
anti-	against	**anti**freeze
circum-, circ	around	**circ**uit
de-	from	**de**frost
dia-	through	**dia**meter
en-	in	**en**danger
extra-	beyond	**extra**ordinary
fore-	before	**fore**cast
inter-	between	**inter**rupt
out-	out; beyond	**out**burst
over-	over	**over**board
post-	after	**post**pone
pre-	before	**pre**caution
super-	above	**super**vise
trans-	across	**trans**port
under-	beneath	**under**age

SUFFIX LIST

THE THREE SOUNDS OF –ED

ed = /ed/	ed = /d/	ed = /t/
rented	sailed	fished
handed	billed	looked
dented	opened	soaked

Suffix	Meaning	Example and Definition
able, ible	capable of (adjective suffix)	**portable** = able to be carried, **legible** = able to be read
ac, ic	like, pertaining to	**cardiac** = pertaining to the heart, **aquatic** = pertaining to the water
acious, icious	full of	**audacious** = full of daring, **avaricious** = full of greed
al	pertaining to	**maniacal** = insane, portal doorway, **logical** = pertaining to logic
ant, ent	full of	**eloquent** = pertaining to fluid, effective speech
ary	like, connected with	**dictionary** = book connected with words
ate	to make (verb suffix)	**consecrate** = to make holy mitigate to make less severe
ation	that which is (noun suffix)	**exasperation** = irritation, annoyance
cy	state of being (noun suffix)	**democracy** = government ruled by people
eer, er, or	person who (noun suffix)	**mutineer** = person who rebels **practitioner** = person who teaches **censor** = person who deletes improper remarks
escent	becoming (adjective suffix)	**evanescent** = tending to vanish **pubescent** = arriving at puberty
fic	making, doing (adjective suffix)	**terrific** = arousing great fear
fy	to make (verb suffix)	**magnify** = enlarge **petrify** = turn to stone
iferous	producing, bearing (adjective suffix)	**pestiferous** = carrying disease **vociferous** = having a loud voice
il, ile	pertaining to, capable of(adjective suffix)	**civil** = polite
ism	doctrine, belief (noun suffix)	**monotheism** = belief in one god

ist	dealer, doer (noun suffix)	**realist** = one who is realistic
ity	state of being (noun suffix)	**sagacity** = wisdom
ive	like (adjective suffix)	**quantitative** = concerned with number or volume
ize, ise	to make (verb suffix)	**harmonize** = make harmonious **enfranchise** = make free
oid	resembling, like (adjective suffix)	**ovoid** = like an egg anthropoid resembling a human being
ose	full of (adjective suffix)	**verbose** = full of words
osis	condition (noun suffix)	**psychosis** = diseased mental condition
ous	full of (adjective suffix)	**nauseous** = full of nausea, ludicrous, foolish
tude	state of (noun suffix)	**fortitude** = state of strength certitude state of sureness

ROOTS: VERBS

Root	Meaning	Example
aud	hear; listen	**aud**ience
cred	believe	in**cred**ible
dic/dict	say; declare	**dict**ionary
duct/duce/duc	lead	con**duct**or
fer	bring; bear; yield	trans**fer**
mem	remember	**mem**ory
mit/mis	send	trans**mit**
pend/pen	hang	**pend**ulum
put	think	dis**put**e
scope	watch; see	tele**scope**
scrib/scrip	write	**scrip**t
spec/spect	watch; see	**spect**ator
tract	pull; drag	**tract**or
vinc/vict	conquer	**vict**ory
vis/vid	see	**vis**ion

ROOTS: NOUNS/DESCRIBING WORDS

Root	Meaning	Example
astro/aster	star	**astro**naut
bio	life	**bio**graphy
cause/cuse/cus	cause/motive	be**cause**
cor/cord/cour	heart	**cour**age
cycl/cyclo	circle	**cycl**one
fin/finis	end	**fin**al
fluc/flu	flowing	**flu**id
forc/fort	strong	**fort**ress
geo	earth	**geo**graphy
leg	law	**leg**al
mar/mer	sea/pool	**mar**sh
mors/mort	death	**mort**al
nov	new	re**nov**ate
ped/pod	foot	**ped**al
poli/polit/polis	city	**polit**ical
sign/signi	sign/mark/seal	**sign**al
terra/terr	earth	**terr**itory
vac	empty	**vac**ant

WORDS OF ORIGIN

When we teach English, we are teaching many languages. Of the over 600,000 words in our language, many are Anglo Saxon, Latin, Greek, or French.

Anglo Saxon words make up 20-25% of the English language. They are the most commonly used words. While they are simple to understand, they are often difficult to read and spell.

- There are vowel teams that are hard to remember and other unusual spellings.

ee: meet   ea: meat

(ea has three different sounds: /ē/ *eat*, /ā/ *steak*, /ĕ/ *head*)

- With the word *hill*, only one final consonant *l* is heard, but it must be spelled with two *l*'s.

Latin words make up about 55% of the English language. They are often multisyllabic words and the meanings can be abstract. There are very few vowel teams to memorize and many vowels are long and easy to pronounce. Most importantly, students begin to read these words in subject matter content areas by 4th grade.

THE DIAGNOSTIC AND PRESCRIPTIVE ELEMENTS OF ORTON-GILLINGHAM

INTRODUCTION TO THE CONCEPT OF SCOPE AND SEQUENCE

Every student is an individual with his or her own unique learning style. The Orton-Gillingham practitioner bases all instruction on this tenet. "One size cannot fit all students" is the motto that practitioners follow. Therefore, it must be understood that there is no one official scope (roadmap) and sequence (order of the roadmap) to follow when developing the instruction and materials for a student. The educator who is truly Orton-Gillingham trained understands how language develops from the simple sound/symbol association of the consonants to the complexities of comprehension and written expression and can see where a student needs to begin or continue on this learning path. When remedial reading programs offer a strict scope and sequence, or a rigid and unbendable list of steps, they are not basing learning on the needs of the student.

There are some common-sense decisions that all practitioners will follow, like starting a very young student with the letter shapes and corresponding sounds of the letters, and moving from one syllable words to two syllable words. But ultimately, every decision made by the practitioner is based on the individual student. The practitioner needs to ask, "What concept should I introduce next, and why would it make sense to present it now?"

The following is a basic scope and sequence to follow for the introduction of phonograms and concepts. How quickly progress is made is fully dependent upon how quickly the students grasps each phonogram, rule, syllable and syllable division type, and generalization.

Sample Scope and Sequence

Letter	Sound	Keyword	Phrase
m	/m/	monkey	
a	/ă/	apple	
t	/t/	turtle	Mat
s	/s/	sun	Mat sat
b	/b/	ball	Tab sat
f	/f/	fish	fat bat
c	/k/	cat	fat cat
i	/ĭ/	igloo	Sit Mat.
h	/h/	hat	fat ham
n	/n/	nut	tin man
p	/p/	pig	pit pat
Concept of a syllable			
Closed Syllable		*CVC* pattern	cat, met, sit, hot, cup,
d	/d/	dog	tan dog
g	/g/	gum	hot gum
r	/r/	rat	big rat
o	/ŏ/	octopus	hot pot
j	/j/	jam	big jam
l	/l/	lion	lap nap
u	/ŭ/	umbrella	sun hat
w	/w/	wagon	wig wag
k	/k/	kite	Kim can
e	/ĕ/	egg	pet pig
y	/y/	yo-yo	Sam the yam.
v	/v/	van	red van
x	/ks/	box	Fox on the box.
qu	/kw/	queen	Quit it.
z	/z/	zebra	zip-zap
Initial Consonant Blends			
bl	/bl/	block	black block
cl	/kl/	clock	click clock
fl	/fl/	flag	flip flap
gl	/gl/	glove	big glove
pl	/pl/	plane	red plane
sl	/sl/	slide	slip slap

sc	/sk/	scale	scat cat
sk	/sk/	skate	skit scat
sm	/sm/	smile	a small smile
sn	/sn/	snail	snap the snail
sp	/sp/	spoon	a moon spoon
sw	/sw/	swing	swim swam
tw	/tw/	twin	twisting twins
br	/br/	brown	a brown brow
cr	/cr/	crab	crunch the crab
dr	/dr/	drum	a drop on the drum
fr	/fr/	frog	a French frog
gr	/gr/	grapes	grab the grapes
pr	/pr/	present	prop the present
tr	/tr/	tree	trot to the tree
scr	/skr/	scream	scream while you scrub
spl	/spl/	splash	splat and splash
spr	/spr/	spring	spring the sprig
shr	/shr/	shrimp	shred the shrimp
squ	/skw/	square	squirt the square
sch	/sk/	school	a schooner school
str	/str/	string	a strip of string
thr	/thr/	thread	thrifty thread
Final consonant blends			
-ct	/kt/	act	an insect in the act
-ft	/ft/	raft	drift on the raft
-lt	/lt/	melt	melt on the pelt
-nt	/nt/	dent	dent in the rent
-pt	/pt/	slept	slept and wept
-lb	/lb/	bulb	hold the bulb
-ld	/ld/	cold	Sold the cold milk.
-lf	/lf/	elf	elf on the shelf
-lm	/lm/	film	Film the elm tree.
-lp	/lp/	help	Help me gulp the pulp.
-mp	/mp/	lamp	Put the stamp on the lamp.
-sp	/sp/	clasp	Clasp the
-sk	/sk/	desk	a disk on the desk
-st	/st/	cast	cast the mast

-xt	/kst/	next	next text
flØss rule- ff, ll, ss, zz			*double f, l, s and sometimes z at the end of a one syllable word right after a short vowel*
-ff	/f/	cuff	his cuff
-ll	/l/	bell	bell in the well
-ss	/s/	pass	pass the mess
-zz	/z/	jazz	a buzz of jazz
-all	/ôl/	ball	fall with the ball
-ck rule	/k/	duck	duck in the truck
-tch rule	/ch/	witch	witch in a ditch
- dge rule	/j/	edge	edge of the ledge
ch	/ch/	chair	chip chop
th- voiced	/th/	mother	this that
wh	/hw/	whale	wham bam
sh	/sh/	shell	ship shop
Magic E syllable (Silent-E)	a-e cake =/ā/ e-e Pete = /ē/ i-e lime = /ī/ o-e bone = /ō/ u-e tube = /ōō/ u-e cube = /ū/ y-e = type = /ī/		bake a cake Give these to Pete. cut the lime dog's bone ride the tube ice cube type the note
wild, kind, old, colt words			
-ild	/īld/	wild	wild child
-ind	/īnd/	kind	kind find
-old	/ōld/	old	old gold
-olt	/ōlt/	colt	bolt the colt.
-ost	/ōst/	host	post the most
VC/CV syllable division			nap/kin, ban/dit, gam/bit, mag/net
Soft c /	/s/	cent	a cent
Soft g	/j/	gem	gold gem
-ng	/ng/	rang, ring, song	bing, bang and bong
-nk	/nk/	ank, ink, onk, unk	sink, sank, honk and plunk
VC/CCV – VCC/CV division			pil/grim ath/lete os/trich

Open syllable	Long vowel sound	/ā/ ba/by /ē/ he/ro /ī/ spi/der /ō/ clo/ver /ū/ mu/sic /ōō/ tu/na /ī/ cry /ē/ candy	lazy baby Mike's hero silent spider no clover pupil's music student's tuna why cry yummy candy
y (vowel)	/ē/	candy	dandy candy
y (vowel)	/ī/	cry	shy cry
y (vowel)	/ĭ/	gym	handy gym
V/CV syllable division			ti/ger, tu/lip, lo/cate
-s, -ing, -ly, -ful, ness, -ment			suns, ring**ing**, shy**ly**, help**ful**, full**ness**, ship**ment**
-less, -est			hope**less**, fast**est**
-ed	/ed/, /t/, /d/	planted = /ed/ jumped = /t/ sailed = /d/	He **jumped** in his boat and **sailed** away as he **planted** the flag.
s /	/z/	has	his has
VC/V syllable division			cam/el, den/im, cab/in
Consonant + le syllable	-ble, -cle. –dle, -fle, -gle, -kle, -ckle, –ple, -stle, --zle		bubble, uncle, fiddle, ruffle, giggle, ankle, buckle, sample, castle, puzzle
Consonant + le division	**Sounds like /ul/**		*start at the e and count back three letters and divide* ma/ple, star/tle, mar, ble, nee/dle
Vowel team syllable			
ee	/ē/	bee	three bees
ay	/ā/	clay	play with clay
oa	/ō/	goat	a coat on the goat
ai	/ā/	rain	rain on the train
ow /ō/	/ō/	crow	The crow is in the snow.
ea /ē/	/ē/	eagle	
oe /ō/	/ō/	toe	He hurt his toe in the hoe.

oy /oi/	/oi/	boy	The boy ate the soy beans.
oi /oi/	/oi/	coin	Put that coin in the soil.
oo	/ŏŏ/	foot	He shook his foot.
oo	/ōō/	food	The food put him in a good mood.
ow	/ou/	cow	How now brown cow?
ph	/f/	phone	Philip has a new phone.
-igh	/ī/	light	That is a bright light.
R-controlled syllable			*all vowels followed by an R*
ar	/ar/	car	a star on the car
or	/or/	fork	sort the forks
er	/er/	fern	her fern
1-1-1 doubling rule			*one syllable word one short vowel one final consonant + a vowel suffix = double the final consonant to make the vowel short hit + ing = hitting*
E dropping rule (Silent-E)			*words ending in a silent e, drop the e when adding a vowel suffix smile + ing = smiling*
-tion	/shun/	lotion	a portion of lotion
-sion	/shun/	mansion	a mission to the mansion
-sion	/zhun/	television	explosion of the television
ir	/er/	bird	the third bird
ur	/ər/	nurse	The nurse had a purse.
Y changing rule (Y to I)		cherry + s = cherries	*words ending in y change the y to i if there is a consonant before the y*
a schwa	/Ə/	about	all about Alaska
Vowel team syllable continued			
ey	/ē/	money	money for hockey camp
ey	/ā/	grey	grey prey
-ture		picture	picture the nature
ie middle of a word	/ē/	thief	shield the thief
ie end of a word	/ī/	pie	piece of pie
ou	/ou/	mouse	loud mouse

ou	/ōō/	soup	soupy soup
ou	/ŭ/	trouble	double trouble
au	/au/	auto	gaudy auto
aw	/au/	saw	jig saw
ea	/ē/	eagle	eager eagle
ea	/ĕ/	bread	healthy bread
ea	/ā/	steak	great steak
eigh	/ā/	eight	eight sleighs
ue	/ōō/	true	true blue
ue	/ū/	rescue	rescue the statue
ew	/ū/	few	a few nephews
ew	/ōō/	grew	chew the stew
or	/er/	doctor	the inventor doctor
eu	/ū/	Europe	a feud in Europe
eu	/ōō	neutral	Eugene is neutral.
ar	/ər/	dollar	a standard dollar
ui	/ōō/	fruit	juicy fruit
Accenting rules			
2-1-1 doubling		permit + ed = permitted	
V/V **syllable division**			li/on mu/se/um ne/on
war	/wer/	homeward	homeward bound
war	/wor/	ward	hospital ward
TEACH AS NEEDED			
u	/ŏŏ/	push	push the bush
-alk		talk	walk the talk
-alt		salt	salty malt
-augh vs -ough			laugh, taught, cough, bought. fought, bough
ch	/k/	chromosome	six chromosomes
ch	/sh/	chef	French Chef
wa	/wô/	water	clear water
qua	/ô/	squash	yellow squash
x	/gz/	exit	exit sign
-que vs -gue		antique, league	an antique league
-se	/z/	nose	a rose on the nose

-se	/s/	chase	a chase on the base
air	/air/	hair	pair of chairs
oar	/or/	boar	a coarse oar
-oor	/or/	moor	The door is on the floor.
-eer	/ēr/	pioneer	Three cheers for the pioneer.
-ear	/ēr/	hear	I fear the lion is near.
-ear	/air/	bear	I swear I hear a bear.
-ear	/ĕr/	heard	I heard the earth shake.
-ear	/ar/	hearth	Put the wood on the hearth.
-our	/our/	hour	Jack will devour the sour apple.
-our	/er/	journey	We will encourage the journey.
-our	/or/	tour	We will tour the exhibit.
-our	/or/	course	He ran the course.
wor	/er/	word	We will worship the winner.
arr	/ăr/	arrow	straight arrow
err	/ĕr/	berry	strawberry patch
irr	/ĭr/	mirror	Look in the mirror.
orr	/ŏr/	borrow	borrow
gn	/n/	gnat	gnarly gnat
-mb	/m/	comb	comb the lamb
-mn	/m/	column	autumn column
gh	/g/	ghost	ghastly ghost
-gh	/f/	laugh	cough and laugh
wr	/r/	write	write with your wrist
kn	/n/	kneel	kneel on my knees
i	/ē/	patio	on the patio with my radio
o	/ŭ/	mother	mother and brother

Introduction to The Multisensory Elements of the Orton-Gillingham Lesson

Visual-Auditory-Kinesthetic-Tactile

Dr. Orton's Language Triangle

Every Orton-Gillingham Lesson is created and presented using direct instruction that integrates the visual, auditory, and kinesthetic/tactile elements.

The visual element allows the student to perceive the physical shape of the letter presented. This is not just the ability to see the letter, but the ability for the brain to create a visual image that can be remembered.

The auditory element enables the student to connect the physical shape of the letter to its corresponding sound. This is not just the ability to hear the sound, but also to be able to distinguish the unique sound of each letter. The student with auditory processing deficits has difficulty gaining automaticity between the visual and auditory elements.

The kinesthetic/tactile element occurs when the student uses the physical actions of tracing and writing to join the elements of visual and auditory input. The dyslexic individual needs the physical component to help in the proficient sequencing of speech sounds. It is important to note that the idea of the kinesthetic element relates to all physical interactions with oral and printed language. Whether the student is tracing with his fingers on a textured surface, writing with a pencil, tapping out sounds for the blending drill, or typing on a keyboard, he is utilizing the physicality of his body to integrate the visual and auditory elements. Another crucial component of the kinesthetic element is the use of the speech organs, which include the placement of the

66

tongue and movement of the lips, to create the appropriate sounds to match the corresponding letters.

The Orton-Gillingham lesson is organized to create the **Language Triangle**, **V-A-K-T**, where the visual, auditory, and kinesthetic elements come together.

INTEGRATION OF HANDWRITING

The ability to take a pencil and create letters on a page is a crucial element in the ability to communicate. It is the kinesthetic link of the VAKT. During initial assessment, the practitioner will be able to immediately see whether students can create the letters they are trying to write.

The student who gains automaticity in handwriting will find it easier to spell because the letters join together to form syllables and words. In addition, writing practice generally reduces the reversals that can happen when students mix up letters like *b* and *d*.

Ultimately, it is best if a student can write in cursive because the pencil point never leaves the surface of the paper. The pencil glides and blends the letters together at the same time the student is trying to blend the sounds together. When students print, the fluency of writing decreases because the pencil point must be lifted off the page when one letter is completed and the next one is formed. The student may often have difficulty spacing letters proficiently, disrupting the ability to spell.

 Handwriting should be taught systematically by the initial letter stroke and not by the sequence of the alphabet. Throughout the lesson, the student should sit up straight with both feet firmly on the floor. It is essential that the student have an appropriate tripod grip when writing. The wrist must be straight in order to provide the student with proper control of the pencil. While the student writes, his non-dominant hand should rest on the paper to keep it from moving. Most occupational therapists suggest using a pencil grip as the student is beginning to learn how to form letters.

The writing paper is not positioned directly in front of the student. Rather, it is placed at an angle of about 45 degrees. The left-handed student turns the paper to the opposite position of the right-handed student. The younger student should use lined paper with lines that are wider and more noticeable. The lines can be in different colors to help the student to determine the top, midpoint, and bottom of the letter.

The pencil used should be of normal width. Overly thick pencils will make the formation of the letters more difficult for the younger child with small hands. Ultimately, the physical writing of the letters is the kinesthetic/tactile link with the visual and auditory components of the VAKT. That is why younger children should be tracing letter shapes on a desk top, a blackboard, or a whiteboard.

INTRODUCTION TO FLUENCY, OR BLENDING, OF SOUNDS

Perhaps the greatest challenge for the student is the ability to blend individual letter sounds into complete syllables and words. If the student is not able to join sounds with automaticity, the therapist/practitioner must bring in multisensory elements. The visual element is immediately created with the letters of the word placed together. The auditory element must now be closely linked to the physical element. For many students, this is done through finger spelling or tapping on a textured surface/table.

A beginning drill that involves the physical element of tapping on the table looks like this:

The student sees a word on a card placed on the tabletop. If the student is right-handed, he will place his hands on the table and tap with his left hand while tracing the letters with his right hand and saying the sound that corresponds to the letter moving in a left to right direction starting with the pinky.

If the student is left-handed, he will tap with his right hand while tracing the letters with his left hand, providing the sound the letter makes moving in a left to right direction starting with the thumb.

CVC CCVC CVCC

CVC pattern (consonant vowel consonant)
/k/ + /ă/ + /t/ = *cat*

CCVC pattern (initial consonant blend in *CVC*)
/f/ + /l/ + /ă/ + /t/ = *flat*

CVCC pattern (final consonant blend in *CVC*)
/f/ + /ă/ + /s/ + /t/ = *fast*

Both consonants in a consonant blend keep their own sound and are tapped out individually.

However, a digraph is two consonants that together make a new sound. They are tapped together.

/sh/ + /ĭ/ + /p/ = ship

Common consonant digraphs are: *sh, wh, th, ch, tch, dge*

Simultaneous Oral Spelling (SOS) is when the student says the name of each letter (not its sound) as it is written. This can be the final step after segmenting the word by its sound on the opposite hand of the writing hand.

Remember: Left-handed students tap with the right hand.
Right-handed students tap with the left hand.

ERROR CORRECTION

Sometimes the OG practitioner will feel that most of each lesson is made up of correcting student errors. That is due to the fact that the OG lesson is an interactive process that guides the student through the concept of self-correction. Students learn how to recognize and correct errors and this is key to developing reading fluency. The goal is to have the student automatically self-correct, as well as have errors decrease in frequency.

During each lesson, the practitioner must quickly indicate that an error has been made. The practitioner may give a clue to the student that an error exists. Then the student must determine how to correct the error. Just as a practitioner should learn the type of errors that take place, so must the student learn them as well.

When the error involves the spelling of a word, the student does not erase or darken out the error. Instead, the student can just draw a line through the error and write the correct spelling above or below it. This allows the student to have the opportunity to review what was written and look over the errors that were made and corrected.

Here is a list of the most common types of errors that happen during the reading of a passage or while spelling a word.

Type of Error	Example
reversals (**b/d**)	*bad* instead of *dad*
rotations (**b/p**)	*back* instead of *pack*
sound confusion	*bit* instead of *bet*
rule based	*cub* instead of *cube*
additions	*plant* instead of *pant*
deletions	*pant* instead of *plant*
transpositions	*on* instead of *no*
whole word substitutions	*shook* instead of *shack*

THE ORTON-GILLINGHAM LESSON PLAN

The Orton-Gillingham lesson plan is a cumulative, structured, systematic lesson plan that is created only after the previous lesson has been taught. It applies the diagnostic/prescriptive principles of OG that keep it an approach vs. a method or program. There are no prescribed lesson plans to be delivered. Each lesson plan is determined by the previous lesson and where the student's errors occurred. Each lesson provides the framework for the next.

Approach vs. Method/Program

Approach

Julia Childs

tailored to what the individual needs and not what he/she doesn't need

Method/Program

Betty Crocker

what is good for one is good for all

Orton-Gillingham is an approach that is tailored to what the individual student needs. Its derivatives are methods/programs in which the lesson is more generic rather than tailored and follows the idea that what is good for one is good for all.

OG lesson plans start with the simple (sound/symbol relationships) and move to the complex (oral reading) with hierarchal steps in between. The main emphasis of the lesson plan is the review and reinforcement section of the lesson. Each lesson is between 45-60 minutes in length.

Each Orton-Gillingham lesson that is created is based upon previously taught phonograms/concepts. The practitioner determines when the student is ready to be introduced to a new phonogram/concept.

The Warm-Up

Every lesson should begin with a quick, 2 to 3 minute handwriting warm-up. This could consist of a cursive or manuscript writing exercise, such as writing the alphabet with eyes closed or averted, writing days of the week/months of the year, etc. This warm-up allows the student to prepare for the writing components of the lesson.

The Drill Pack

The drill pack is the means by which the practitioner can review past concepts using the VAKT language triangle. The drill pack portion of the lesson allows the practitioner to determine if the student has developed automaticity of sound/symbol relationships. Drill packs ideally contain 12-15 phonogram cards although there might be more. All drill packs have the short vowel phonogram cards as a constant while the rest of the drill pack is fluid depending upon phonograms/concepts recently introduced and mastered phonograms/concepts being reviewed.

The Visual Drill

For the visual drill, the practitioner holds the card pack in the palm of one hand and flips the cards with the other hand as quickly as the student can read the sound of the symbol on the card and trace on a rough surface with the index and middle fingers of their writing hand. If more than one sound of a letter has been introduced to the student, they are expected to give the sounds they know in their order of frequency (this is found on the back of the card). For example, if the practitioner has introduced both the soft and hard sound of *c*, then the student is expected to give the two sounds - /k/ and /s/ while tracing only the *c*. Depending on the needs of the student, the student can give just the sound(s) represented by the symbol, or they can give the name of the letter on the card, a key word, and then the sound. This is done for each card in the drill pack until all the cards have been presented.

If the student has difficulty providing the sound of the phonogram, the student should be given a little time to see if they can produce the sound(s). The student should trace the letter again on the rough surface to see if that activates their memory of the sound. A **visual clue** can also be given by writing a word beginning with or containing the phonogram (*x* – fo*x*). A hand signal can help for short vowel sounds and digraphs; pointing to a picture or color can also be used. Whatever is used should be quick and efficient. Once the student has the sound, they should trace the letter while simultaneously producing the sound three times. Then the phonogram card is returned to the deck for immediate reinforcement. The practitioner makes a note that this phonogram needs further reinforcement.

The **VAKT** components of the visual drill are:
- **visual** – seeing the phonogram on the card
- **auditory** – the student hearing him/herself produce the sound(s)
- **kinesthetic/tactile** – tracing the letter formation on a rough surface with the index and middle fingers

THE AUDITORY DRILL

Using the same drill pack as used in the visual drill, the practitioner quickly shuffles the pack so that the order is not the same. The student needs a piece of paper folded in half length-wise ("hot dog") if the student's handwriting size allows it, so the student can utilize two columns of the paper. If the handwriting size is too large, the paper is not folded. The student should skip lines as he/she works down the paper. The practitioner holds the cards so that the student cannot see the phonogram on the card. The practitioner gives the sound on the card, and the student echoes/repeats the sound dictated and writes the letter of the sound on the line. If there are multiple spellings for the sound that have been taught, then the student writes the spellings in the order of frequency (see the back of the drill card for the order). For example, if the practitioner has introduced four ways to spell the long *a* sound /ā/, then the student would write *a*, *a-e*, *ai*, *ay*. Each sound is given only one time as each line on the piece of paper the student is writing on represents the spelling(s) of a sound dictated. For example, if you already dictated /k/ with the *-ck* card, do not give the /k/ sound for the *c* card; skip it and any other card that says /k/. If the student writes the wrong letter(s) but self-corrects, have the student cross out the incorrect letter and rewrite – **students should never erase any of their work**. The auditory drill continues until each card in the pack has been presented.

If the student has difficulty giving the spelling(s) of the phonogram, the student should be given a short time to see if he/she can produce the spelling(s) of the sound. The practitioner can demonstrate way the sound is produced (this is most helpful for auditory discrimination of /f/ and /th/). Whether the sound is voiced or unvoiced can be discussed. An **auditory clue** can be given by saying a word or two which uses the sound(s). Once the student has the spelling, the student can trace the letter(s) while simultaneously producing the sound three times. The phonogram card is returned to the deck for immediate reinforcement. The practitioner makes a note that this phonogram needs further reinforcement.

The VAKT components of the auditory drill are:
- **visual** – seeing the letter(s) written on the sheet of paper
- **auditory** – the practitioner producing the sound and the student echoing/repeating the sound
- **kinesthetic/tactile** – writing the letter(s) on the sheet of paper

THE BLENDING DRILL

In this drill, the goal is for the student to gain automaticity, which will lead to reading fluency. The student must combine visual letter shapes with the corresponding sounds to build syllables and words.

During this drill, the phonogram cards are quickly placed on the tabletop. For the student blending cvc words, the vowel cards are placed in the middle, with the initial and final consonant cards placed to the left and right. The practitioner will manipulate the cards and quickly flip letters to immediately form real and nonsense words, depending on what card is flipped next.

cat	bat	bit	bot	sot	sit	mit

Different activities, such as phonological awareness, syllable activities, or sight word work can also be used depending upon the student's area of need.

REVIEW AND REINFORCEMENT

This part of the lesson is the heart of the lesson. It is a cumulative review of all previously taught phonograms/concepts through words to read, words to spell, phrases/sentences to read, and phrases/sentences to spell.

WORDS TO READ

The student will read aloud a group of **20-30** words containing the sounds in the current drill pack and any other previously taught phonograms/concepts. Fewer words may be warrented depending upon the student's reading efficiency and fluency. If syllables have been introduced, some two-syllable words for reading can be incorporated. Multi-syllables can be added for an advanced student.

WORDS TO SPELL

Give the student a new piece of paper, folding it in half length-wise ("hot dog") so that words can be written on both halves of the paper. The student does not number the lines but does skip lines as words are written. The practitioner dictates, and the student echoes back the word prior to writing. The practitioner will dictate between 10-20 words.

If the student has difficulty with sequencing the sounds in the word dictated, seems unsure, or misspells the word, have the student finger spell (as described on p. 69) after crossing out the misspelled word. After segmenting these sounds and symbols, the student will use Simultaneous Oral Spelling (SOS) to say the name of each letter as they write the letters. After the student rewrites the word correctly, the practitioner should dictate three additional words that focus on the missed phonogram/concept. For example, if the practitioner dictates *stuck* and the student writes *stuk*, three more words should be given with -ck (*click, black, duck*) using fingerspelling/tapping and SOS. Multi-syllable words can be broken apart by syllables or by prefixes, roots, and suffixes. If syllables have been introduced, some two-syllable words can be incorporated for spelling. Multisyllables can be added for an advanced student. When the dictation is completed, the student reads back all the words.

PHRASES/SENTENCES TO READ AND SPELL

Next the student should be given one or two phrases/sentences each to read and write which contain sounds that are still troublesome, making sure all rules/concepts are observed. The sentences to read can be written on a piece of paper, a sentence strip, a white board, etc. This is a good time to work on phrasing within the sentence to improve fluency. When the sentence is dictated, the student should echo or repeat back the whole sentence before writing it on the same sheet of paper that the words to spell were written on. If the student needs more than one line to write the sentence, they should still skip lines. If the student writes the whole phrase/sentence but had difficulty spelling a word in the phrase/sentence, have the student cross out the misspelled word, and on the line above or below, rewrite the word using the strategies described in the words to spell section (fingerspelling/tapping, SOS, etc.). When phrases/sentences are completed, have the student reread them aloud.

The practitioner should avoid reusing the same words in different parts of the lesson. However, if a word must be reused, the modality should be switched. For example, if you used the word *stretch* for a word to read, then use *stretch* in a sentence to spell.

A special reinforcement exercise, such as a special chart or some type of structured exercise or game focused on a spelling pattern, syllable, or other language concept can be used in this part of the lesson.

NEW INFORMATION

Using the sequence and weaknesses found in the student's testing and assessments, the next phonogram or concept is presented here. When introducing a new concept, the practitioner will show the phonogram card and keep it visible throughout the introduction. The practitioner gives the sound the letter(s) represent, has the student repeat it, and then provides a key word. If there is a rule/generalization that accompanies the phonogram, the practitioner will discuss the rule/generalization. The student traces the letter(s) on a rough surface with the index and middle fingers, simultaneously saying the name of the letter(s) as it is traced and then gives the sound it represents. This is repeated three times. If appropriate, the practitioner can discuss the "feel" of the sound in the student's throat and mouth, using a mirror if needed. Other kinesthetic cues can be discussed, such as voiced or unvoiced sounds. The practitioner will provide eight to ten words that use the new phonogram/concept. The student can underline or highlight the phonogram in each word first before reading the words. Four to six words that are then dictated that contain the new information. These words will be written on a fresh sheet of paper, and the student reads back the words after writing them. Present the phonogram card and ask the student to give the sound and rules of usage. This card will be added to the existing drill pack, and the practitioner will include words containing this phonogram/ concept in the review and reinforcement section of future lessons until the phonogram is mastered. Conclude this part of the lesson by having the student restate the phonogram/concept introduced.

ORAL READING

Oral reading is the culmination of all the teaching the student has received 5-10 minutes at the end of a 45-minute lesson, or 10-15 minutes at the end of a 60-minute lesson. will expect the following skills. The oral reading should ideally be a time where the student feels a satisfaction with his or her achievement of reading. Focus should be on the following skills:

- accurate decoding
- natural language - for example, read *the* as /thə/ not /thē/
- using the natural cadence of the language, not a monotone
- phrasing – students can shown (or taught) how punctuation gives signals for pauses (commas and semicolons), stops (periods and colons), and inflection (question marks and exclamation points)
- when a passage has been read, the text should be discussed with the student checking for comprehension; you may have chosen some good comprehension questions during the reading time; also, before the daily reading begins, you may set the stage or review what has already; for older students who are reading longer passages, the comprehension exercises that follow the reading may include note-taking or completing graphic organizers

The practitioner chooses or creates phonetically-appropriate reading material for the student. There will be some words the student will not be responsible for; the practitioner will give the student these words as they are encountered in reading. The student must be held accountable for phonograms/concepts learned and expected to divide words and use syllable types as decoding strategies. Guessing is discouraged since the emphasis is an alphabetic approach - *"Being permitted, even encouraged to guess a word that 'will fit into the story' is one of the most devastating experiences encountered by the language-disabled student"* (The Gillingham Manual, p. 96).

KEEPING THE LESSON DIAGNOSTIC AND PRESCRIPTIVE

Even after disgnosis of the student's difficulties and embarkement on activities for remediation, it is important to keep an accurate record of what the student is learning and how it is being retained. Because Orton-Gillingham is an approach in which all lessons are tailor-made to the particular learner, this can be accomplished only through diligent effort to keep track of this information.

- Student should include the **date** on each sheet of paper so that progress, or regression, can be noted accurately.
- In the drill, **the student should repeat the sound**, and in the dictation of words and sentences, **the student should repeat the word(s)** to make sure that he/she heard what was said. The student may hear all the sounds correctly but put them in the wrong order or insert or delete a sound. These errors must be noted.
- In the visual and auditory drill, **the cards the student had difficulty with should be put in a separate pile** so they can be reviewed immediately before moving onto the next part of the lesson, and so they can be noted for the subsequent lesson.
- After the lesson, words the student struck through should be evaluated for problem phonograms or rules.
- Use 〰〰〰 to **mark out practitioner errors** such as when a word was included that the student should not be responsible for decoding or encoding at the present level.
- A note should be made of **retired/mastered phonograms or concepts in the Drill or Review and Reinforcement** misspelled or mispronounced. These should be reviewed and reinforced in the next lesson.
- **Miscalled words in Oral Reading** will indicate which phonemes and concepts are making the transition from isolated work to the student's repertoire of word attack strategies.
- Put the **sequence chart** (discussed later in this guide) in the student's notebook for an instant update.

THE STUDENT NOTEBOOK

The Orton-Gillingham Approach reminds practitioners that teaching must be individualized to meet the needs of each student. The presentation of content will vary and change as the student is introduced to new concepts.

 A vital component to instruction is the need to check for a student's understanding of concepts previously introduced. This is why the Student Notebook is a crucial part of a student's instruction. Usually, the notebook is a three-ring binder where pages can be added as new concepts are introduced.

The notebook allows the practitioner to remind the student and parent when a new concept is introduced and which concepts must be reviewed. To help facilitate this, a checkoff list is placed at the front of the notebook so the practitioner, the parent, and the student can keep track of concepts previously introduced. In addition, homework materials are located in the front pocket so students can easily find them and begin working.

After each instructional session, the student must drill and practice new concepts, while also reviewing older concepts. Seeing a practitioner two or three times each week will not help the student to develop automaticity. Multisensory instruction requires daily practice until the next instructional session, so the practitioner can decide if the student is comprehending new material while also becoming proficient when using it in reading and writing activities.

The parent plays a crucial part in the success of the student. Just like homework assignments from the classroom must be completed, so must the OG drills. The parent can also help to clarify for the practitioner when the student is having difficulty understanding or using a new concept when reading and writing.

Most importantly, the student notebook is the history of the student's OG education. If the student moves to a new location or begins work with a new practitioner, the notebook will provide the diagnostic and prescriptive information that the new practitioner will need in order to help keep the student on track.

The notebook contains sections that change as the student continues to learn new concepts. The younger student often likes to participate in decorating and setting up new sections. This interaction will help the student to stay motivated about learning new skills because the notebook shows how much has been accomplished.

Suggested Order of Introduction in the Student Notebook:

Fluency and Spelling
- Checkoff List of Previously Introduced Concepts
- Current Homework/Drill
- Phonogram Sounds
- The Six Syllables
- Syllabication Rules
- Spelling Rules
- Sight Words
- Affixes/Vocabulary
- Spelling Drill
- Dictation Drill
- Reading Passages

Comprehension/Writing
- Current Homework/Drill
- Grammar:
    o Parts of Speech
    o Sentence Structure
    o Paragraph Structure
- Affixes/Vocabulary
- Writing:
    o Paragraphs
    o Short Answer Format
    o Essay Format

- o Story Format
- Comprehension
  - o Fiction Passages
  - o Nonfiction Passages

Understanding the Needs of the Individual Student

The Student Profile

Just as the medical doctor must have a thorough medical history of a new patient before the correct treatment is determined, the educator must also have a thorough educational history of the new student before appropriate instruction is initiated. The key terms to use in both cases are *diagnostic* and *prescriptive*.

Both a doctor and the OG educator must look at past testing results and narratives written about the patient/student. This is the area of assessment. Both the doctor and the practitioner will conduct testing of their own in order to develop a more exact level of treatment. When the past testing information is combined with the new data collected, the doctor and the educator can diagnosis where the patient/student should begin new treatment. This is now the prescriptive part of the process. Where should the patient/student be taken next?

Unfortunately, in education, the practitioner is rarely trained in the area of assessment and has little knowledge of what types of testing tools can be utilized. Often, a new student is placed in a classroom and the practitioner is provided with little information. Also, many practitioners are not trained to understand the results documented in the student's IEP narrative or psycho-educational evaluation, nor are they aware of appropriate instructional materials.

The Orton-Gillingham approach advocates a diagnostic and prescriptive plan before instruction begins.

The Student Profile is a written narrative by the instructor/practitioner that begins with the detailing of the student's background information.

MEDICAL HISTORY

The practitioner looks at any issues at birth; including birth weight and respiratory difficulties. It is important to find out if the very young child had any recurring health issues including ear infections, allergies, and asthma. It is also crucial to find out if there were any visual or hearing problems.

Another important area to review are the developmental milestones for speech language acquisition. The practitioner should also look at information on fine/gross motor issues, and attention problems.

Finally, the practitioner needs to know if the student is on medications which could affect the ability to learn.

FAMILY HISTORY

Related to the medical history, the practitioner should look at information about the dynamics of the student's home life. Was the child adopted? Are there any siblings? Is the home bilingual or multilingual? Has the family moved often, which could have affected participation in school? It is also important to find out if there is a history of learning issues in the family.

EDUCATIONAL HISTORY

Has the child received special education services in the past, including speech, occupational and physical therapy, and placement in a self-contained resource room or inclusion classroom? Is there an Individualized Educational Plan (IEP) or 504 Plan for the child due to medical issues like attention deficit disorder? Did the child attend public school, private school, charter school, or was he or she home schooled?

TESTING INFORMATION

The practitioner should look at the student's academic profile, which is made up of classroom tests, grades, and practitioner progress reports and running records. If the child was considered for special services, what standardized testing was conducted by the child study team and what did the results indicate?

PREVIOUS ORTON-GILLINGHAM INSTRUCTION

Has the child received remediation from an Orton-Gillingham program or practitioner prior to the new instruction?

When updating the student profile after the current Orton-Gillingham remediation has begun, the practitioner needs to describe the history of the remediation, including duration, number of sessions per week, and the length of each session. The practitioner should keep a detailed record of what concepts have been previously introduced, including phonograms, syllables, spelling rules, and syllable division rules. The practitioner should describe the student's current learning needs, including areas of strengths and weaknesses.

The Student Profile should be constantly updated. The idea is to have information available for other educators, the parents, or school if the practitioner is unable to continue the practitionerial.

INFORMAL AND FORMAL INSTRUMENTS

The practitioner must have an introduction to the concepts of informal and formal assessments. This will enable the practitioner to develop a Student Profile that will serve as the foundation for a diagnostic/prescriptive Orton-Gillingham remedial program.

An understanding of testing information can help the practitioner better determine the student's potential by knowing the cognitive level of the learner and what possible discrepancies may be prevalent. The practitioner can also develop a baseline on the student's processing ability which includes phonological awareness, visual and auditory strengths and weaknesses, and visual-motor integration.

It is important to note that in some states the term *dyslexia* will not be used in a public-school report due to the fact that these states do not yet recognize *dyslexia* as a legal term. Therefore, it is very important for practitioners to begin to see how the formal testing assessments can still provide the information that is needed to understand the language delays that are affecting their students.

Practitioners must also understand how assessment examiner manuals define the nature of reading and where the term *dyslexia* might be inferred because it is not explicitly stated. Below is a visual that shows the similarities of dyslexia and a specific learning disability, the term that public schools might use, especially in testing.

Dyslexia/Specific Learning Disability
a language-based learning difference

Dyslexia is a specific learning disability that is neurobiological in origin. It is characterized by difficulties with accurate and/or fluent word recognition and by poor spelling and decoding abilities. These difficulties typically result from a deficit in the phonological component of language that is often unexpected in relation to other cognitive abilities and the provision of effective classroom instruction. Secondary consequences may include problems in reading comprehension and reduced reading experience than can impede growth of vocabulary and background knowledge.
-IDA and NICHD-

A disorder in 1 or more of the basic psychological processes involved in understanding or in using language, spoken or written, which disorder may manifest itself in the imperfect ability to listen, think, speak, read, write, spell, or do mathematical calculations.
-IDEA 2004-

phonological processing
visual memory for words and auditory memory for speech sounds

Dyslexia is difficulty in the use and processing of linguistic and symbolic codes, alphabetic letters representing speech sounds, or numeric symbols representing numbers or quantities. Such difficulty is reflected in the language continuum that includes spoken language, written language, and language comprehension.
-AOGPE-

spelling

UNDERSTANDING
or in
USING
LANGUAGE

SPELL

writing

reading

READ

WRITE

handwriting

WRITE

arithmetic

MATHEMATICAL
CALCULATIONS

receptive and expressive language
written and verbal

LISTEN, SPEAK, WRITE,
THINK

Characteristics of dyslexia. (IDA, NICHD, AOGPE)

Characteristics of a "specific learning disability." (IDEA '04)

neurological in origin, often familial, average to above average intelligence
these characteristics form the "backbone" of dyslexia

Heidi High Bishop, Fellow/AOGPE

Knowledge of **informal assessments** can help the practitioner review the student's classroom performance throughout the school year. The practitioner can also learn how to utilize informal assessment when conducting the initial intake of information for a new student.

Furthermore, knowledge of **formal testing measures** will help the practitioner better understand how these standardized tests determine cognitive levels, academic levels, the discrepancies between related skills to help develop the dyslexia/SLD diagnosis.

Some differences in terminology used for informal and formal measures are:

- **Criterion-Referenced** (informal) assessments compare performance to a specific standard or criterion, not to a norm sample.
- **Norm Referenced** (formal) assessments have statistics for comparing students to a large sample of similar students.

In fact, there is no single test or assessment that can independently diagnose dyslexia. Therefore, the practitioner must triangulate the data from:

1. the Case History
2. informal observation and criterion-referenced (informal) assessments conducted in the classroom
3. norm-referenced (formal) testing by the Child Study Team (this team's name might vary state-by-state)

Additionally, assessing a reading problem comes down to two questions:

1. What is the child's reading level and how severe is the reading delay?
2. What is the general area of the reading problem?

To look at the severity issue is to determine the student's current reading level vs. the age/grade appropriate reading level.

Although there are variations, most assessment tools define severe as:

- Grades 1, 2, 3 = One year or more delay
- Grades 4, 5, 6 = Two years or more delay
- Grade 7 & up = Three years or more delay

These reading levels, or degrees of delay, will vary from one assessment tool to the next.

The practitioner must remember that when he/she is collecting data for the Student Profile most assessment tools, both formal and informal, are developed in isolation:

1. The assessment tool may be culturally biased. Some students live in high poverty areas where the home may have little stability or security. Reading materials and enriched learning opportunities may not be available. Some students live in bi-lingual or, even tri-lingual households, where the student with a reading delay is overwhelmed by language.
2. The assessment tool may not consider the student's intelligence/cognitive ability. While the IQ assessment will look directly at this issue, most reading assessments do not consider the issue of how intelligence can affect language development.
3. The assessment tool may not take into consideration that the student has medical differences like Attention Deficit Disorder, emotional disturbance, or Pervasive Disability Disorder on the autistic spectrum.

The practitioner must remember that when compiling data for the Student Profile, he/she must balance testing results with information on the student's social, medical, and educational history.

INFORMAL ASSESSMENTS

Informal Assessments are usually done by the educator "on the front lines" to analyze why the student is not succeeding. Informal assessments can be legally administered by anyone, including classroom practitioners.

With respect to informal assessments, different tests measure different skills, including:

- **Letter Identification** – Child identifies letter names and sounds.
- **Phonological Awareness** – awareness of individual sounds in words.
- **Rapid Automatic Naming (RAN)** – the ability to quickly recognize letters.
- **Letter & Word Identification** – recognizes regular and irregular words.

- **Word Attack** – recognizes nonsense words.
- **Reading Vocabulary** – can provide antonyms, synonyms, analogies.
- **Reading Comprehension** – answering open ended and multiple choice.
- **Fluency and Automaticity** – reading passages while being timed.
- **Listening Comprehension** – answer questions on passages read to the student.

Informal measures are not normed or standardized on large populations.

Informal measures are flexible. Because these tests are not standardized, the practitioner is able to make modifications in test procedures. For example, if a student exhibits loss of focus during the reading of a passage, the practitioner can choose to shorten the amount of reading to decrease the chance that the student gets agitated, which could impact a true assessment of his/her ability.

Informal measures also allow the practitioner to personalize the assessment, for example, by using certain kinds of reading material.

Informal assessments are thought to give a more authentic profile of the student's reading ability because the reading passages utilized are more similar to the actual reading tasks the student will do in school.

An informal reading inventory (IRI) is one type of informal assessment used to assess reading. It is usually a series of graded reading selections followed by questions. These passages are not phonetically controlled. Many also include grade-leveled word lists. The practitioner can use a student's knowledge of word lists to help determine at what grade level to begin testing.

Informal reading inventories require students to read silently and/or orally. Reading orally can help practitioners record reading errors or miscues.

Reading orally also helps:

- The practitioner finds the student's reading level faster. This can help lower student frustration and anxiety.

- The practitioner understands the student's fluency rate (words read correctly per minute).
- Pick up on student miscues like:
  - **substitutions** – replacing letters or words
  - **omissions** – leaving out letters or words
  - **reversals** – turning words around
- Track self-corrections in order to determine the student's ability to self-monitor as she or he reads.

One quick note: mispronunciations resulting from dialect differences, speaking English as a second language, immature speech patterns, or speech impediments do not count as errors.

The final score on the oral reading passage for an informal reading inventory is based on word recognition accuracy and comprehension.

The final score on the silent reading passage is based only on the comprehension score.

The word recognition accuracy score and the comprehension score determine three reading levels:

1. **Independent Level** – at which the student can read without practitioner guidance. Use for recreational reading.
2. **Instructional Level** – at which a student can read with practitioner support. Use this level for reading instruction.
3. **Frustrational Level** – this level is too hard for the student. Avoid this level.

Finally, many informal reading inventories only look at narrative text (story format). However, students may have difficulty with expository text, too (informational text, non-fiction format). If you do use an IRI, use both narrative and expository text.

A few limitations of IRIs:

1. If the practitioner is untrained in using the assessment tool, he or she can mis-score the student's responses.
2. If the practitioner uses a reading passage with content that is familiar to the student or of high interest to the student, it can affect the results. Therefore, it is important to talk with the student as the evaluation begins to better ascertain if a reading passage selected will provide an accurate score.
3. The IRI can sometimes provide reading selections that are too short or simple to provide data.

FORMAL ASSESSMENTS

Formal standardized tests measure reading ability on short passages and multiple-choice answers because many these tests use a large number of subtests to develop a score. As a result, it is quicker and more efficient for the tester to score and analyze. Therefore, many practitioners are concerned that reading fluency is not fully determined because these formal tests don't allow enough time to see if students exhibit oral miscues, which include the omissions of words, the substitution of words, and the reversal of words because the passages are so short.

Formal Tests serve several purposes:

- Allowing educators to compare a student to others of the same age or grade level.
- Providing scores that are used by many professionals.
- Helping practitioners make more objective decisions about a student's performance.
- Fulfilling legal requirements.

Here are some terms used when using formal assessments:

- **Raw Score** – the number correct on the test.
- **Derived Score** –converted from the raw score and used to interpret the student's performance.

- **Normal Distribution Curve** – shows how many students earned particular scores on tests with most scores falling in the middle.
- **Grade Equivalent** – indicates how a student performs in term of grade level.

Validity refers to whether a test measures what it is supposed to measure. There are two types of validity with respect to tests.

1. **Content Validity** - inspecting the test to see whether the items are valid for testing purposes.

   Example: A valid reading comprehension test should contain passages with questions.

2. **Criterion Validity** - how the test compares with some other aspects of achievement.

   Example: Comparing a score to the corresponding grade point average.

Reliability refers to the stability of test scores. If a test is reliable, child being tested will receive the same score on repeated test administrations.

The classroom teacher and the Child Study Team (or whatever this team is named in a particular state or school district) members must communicate on a regular basis. Too often, the Child Study Team members have little, or no knowledge, of the actual curriculum being utilized in the classroom. They only enter the classroom to observe a student when testing is being conducted. Ultimately, they are developing the student profile/narrative in isolation.

The classroom teacher usually has little training in basic assessment and is not able to utilize testing results in the development of remedial materials. Very often, the classroom practitioner will only skim the student file and not integrate the testing results into classroom instruction.

EXAMPLES OF ASSESSMENT TOOLS

Informal Assessments: Criterion Referenced Tests

- Gallistel – Ellis Test of Coding Skills (GE)
- Yopp-Singer Test of Phoneme Segmentation
- Developmental Spelling Analysis (DSA)
- Words Their Way Inventory
- Ekwall-Shanker Reading Inventory
- Wilson Assessment of Decoding and Encoding (WADE)
- DIBELS
- Developmental Reading Assessment (DRA)
- Rigby Reads
- Informal Reading Inventory (IRI)

Formal Test: Norm Referenced Tests

- Woodcock Johnson IV Tests of Achievement (WJ)
- Wechsler Individual Achievement Test (WIAT)
- Kaufman Test of Educational Achievement (KTEA)
- Wide Range Achievement Test (WRAT)
- Gray Oral Reading 5 (GORT)
- Test of Written Language (TOWL)
- Comprehensive Test of Phonological Processing (CTOPP 2)
- Test of Word Reading Efficiency (TOWRE)
- Test of Phonological Awareness (TOPA 2)
- Phonological Awareness Test (PAT 2)

Going Beyond Phonemic Awareness and Phonics: Grammar, Comprehension, and Writing

Other elements of OG instruction beyond learning and mastering symbol/sound relationships through phonograms, syllables, and syllable division are grammar, comprehension, and writing.

The process of writing is highly related to the process of reading because readers and writers are both constructing or composing meaning. At all levels, practice in writing increases the understanding of how authors compose text. Students also use writing to clarify the meaning of what they read. When they make written responses to reading, they increase comprehension.

Grammar is the foundation!

In order to become proficient readers and writers, students must understand the structure of grammar. Since language is the process by which meanings are exchanged, grammar is the set of rules that describe how to structure language. Traditional grammar is often taught out of sequence, through rote memorization. One week of nouns may be followed by a week of verbs.

The failure to teach the rule structure (grammar) of the language results in students who may decode well but are unable to put their thoughts on paper at a level commensurate with their cognitive abilities, and with others who are struggling to make the language work as a reliable tool for academic learning (Mann, 2006).

Once the reader understands the way multisyllabic words can be formed, and then combined, to create sentences, real comprehension and written expression begin.

In order to become a more proficient reader and writer, the student has to understand the structure of the sentence and the paragraph. At the same time, the student must understand how language forms meaning.

Syntax refers to the word order in sentences:

Bill painted the barn blue.
Bill painted the blue barn.

Semantics refers to word meaning, how words relate to each other, and what words mean in sentences:

New York was the destination for the field trip.
New York was the last stop for the field trip.

Many struggling students have difficulty with enhancing their use of language. These students do not seem to have much to say because they have trouble finding the right words to use when having to analyze or describe something. That is why they must constantly drill and practice developing their language skills. Perhaps the most classic area of remediation is in the use of the descriptors adjectives and adverbs.

Some writing programs suggest creating an adjective and adverb word wall, often based on the five basic senses. As the school year progresses, new descriptive words can be added to the collection. These new words can be generated through reading passages, short stories, and content area subjects like science and social studies. The use of oral language is the key for generating new word choices as it allows the practitioner to view the student's use of language in their expressive language.

Using the example of *lava* (molten matter thrown out by volcanoes, solidifying as it cools), the student may say that lava is hot and seek synonyms, such as *"It is boiling, burning, fiery, red-hot, and scalding,"* or use analogies, such as *"It is like an oven, a furnace, and a thousand exploding suns!"*

Students should avoid the use of the words *nice, good,* and *bad*.

BUILDING THE SENTENCE

In writing a sentence the student should first be aware of the:

naming part	+	action part
noun	+	verb
subject	+	predicate

For example:

The boy	+	runs.

This is called an independent clause. Some writing textbooks call this a sentence kernel.

Add descriptors: adjectives and adverbs

The athletic boy	+	runs quickly.

Add a prepositional phrase:

The athletic boy	+	runs quickly in the park.

Add compound subjects and compound predicates:

The athletic boy and girl	+	run quickly in the park and play baseball.

Add another independent clause and make it into a compound sentence:

The athletic boy and girl	+	run into the park and play baseball, but they do not play basketball.

Change the tense:

The athletic boy and girl	+	ran into the park and played baseball, but they did not play basketball.

THE PARAGRAPH AND EXPOSITORY TEXT

As students grow older, fiction becomes a smaller part of reading, and informational texts become the major source of learning, especially in science and social studies. Students are expected to read a chapter, answer questions, study for tests, participate in class discussions, and write essays about the content they have learned.

However, few elementary school practitioners actually instruct students on how to read and comprehend paragraphs or textbooks.

Expository text conveys information, explains ideas, or presents a point of view. Expository material is usually organized in one of five ways (Englert 1984):

1. **Sequence or time order** – usually used to present history or the "steps in a process" of completing a task.

   Examples:
   World War II
   How to Dissect a Fetal Pig.

2. **Compare and Contrast** – involves discussing similarities and differences.

   Examples:
   Compare Different Types of Government
   Compare Types of Cells

3. **Description** – used to explain the features of an object or event.

Examples:

List the Features of a Reptile

4. **Cause/Effect** – outlines reasons for events.

Examples:

The Fall of the Roman Empire
The Effect of Smoking on the Lungs.

5. **Problem/Solution** – discusses a problem and then suggests possible solutions

Examples:

How a City Reduced Air Pollution

Skilled readers recognize these organizational patterns and use them to build comprehension. However, many expository materials do not conform precisely to the patterns. Often the patterns are intermixed in the writing.

Struggling students have difficulty comprehending expository text because:

1. they have difficulty recognizing the organizational patterns
2. they are forced to take tests to demonstrate understanding of content
3. the texts have more difficult vocabulary and technical terms
4. the texts require background knowledge
5. the texts and reading requirements are much longer
6. the reading level is often at the frustrational level

Finally, many students understand a text while they are reading, but quickly forget it afterward. As a result, they perform poorly on tests. To study effectively, students must transform the text in some way so they can remember it. They must be able to identify and set apart important ideas.

In reading development textbooks designed for struggling students, the structure of the paragraph is dissected. As discussed above, the student benefits from learning about the basic ways that content can be organized. They must learn how to locate the topic sentence or topic words in the paragraph. Once this is accomplished, the student can more easily locate the supporting facts.

 Another strategy to help aid the struggling reader is to introduce the concept of transitional/signal words. Like traffic signals, these words give the reader directions about what is coming up next. They help the reader follow the writer's thinking. In addition, students learn that these words also assist them when they are writing by helping to connect ideas together. Once again, these words can be displayed on a permanent bulletin board or available at the student's desk.

SIGNAL WORDS

Go Words:	Stop Words:
First, Second, Next,	Finally, Last of all,
Then, Also, Later on,	In conclusion, Therefore,
In addition, For example,	As a result,

One Orton-Gillingham based reading program entitled *Project Read*, (Enfield and Greene) advocates having struggling readers outline the paragraphs by boxing in topic words and underlining key facts as they read. Another comprehension textbook entitled *Reasoning and Reading*, (Carlisle) encourages students to circle the signal words that begin many sentences and connect compound sentences.

These ideas follow the multisensory approach that Orton-Gillingham advocates. The student is now actively engaged in the reading process. He/She must pay closer attention, and look to understand what the writer is trying to convey. The reader is now integrating fluency, vocabulary, and the writing patterns that make up the reading selection.

Once the student can better understand how to comprehend a reading passage, and the paragraphs that connect the content together, then he or she can begin to use those same concepts in writing.

WRITING

Writing instruction should start simple and use scaffolding strategies.

Unfortunately, in recent years, standardized testing materials have used a picture prompt to elicit a writing sample. The elementary school pupil is given from thirty minutes to one hour to write a narrative/fictional story to go with the image. As a result, many schools began to approach all reading comprehension and writing opportunities only in the fictional formats. Little time was given to the basics, and children as young as six years of age were worrying about writing stories that included such sophisticated elements as dialogue, simile, metaphors and figurative language.

Too often, students are given a blank page and told to start writing, so they freeze up like a deer in the headlights.

The key to organizing writing is to keep it simple and direct.

Educator and author Diana King, in her workbook, *Writing Skills,* suggests that students simply generate lists. This leads to developing brainstorming abilities and promotes creativity. It also goes hand in hand with the continuing development of vocabulary.

Example of a list:

Topic: Ways to Annoy Your Practitioner

1. ask to go to the bathroom
2. do the wrong math problems
3. during a test on verbs, ask what a verb is

The list is the beginning of the outlining process. It becomes the center/body of the paragraph. It is topped with a topic sentence and followed by the concluding sentence.

THE BIG FIVE PARAGRAPH/THE BASIC PARAGRAPH

The next step for a student when writing a paragraph should be to compose the topic sentence. Then, they should use their lists to write at least three supporting sentences. Each supporting sentence should begin with a signal/transitional word or phrase. Finally, each paragraph should end with a concluding sentence.

Example: The Example Paragraph

There are many fun places to go to for a vacation. First, the beach is a good wonderful place to get some sun. Second, England has funny roads and cars. Finally, Italy has great ice cream. In conclusion, you better start saving your money for your vacation.

As the student continues to practice writing a complete paragraph, from topic sentence to the concluding sentence, he must also practice writing different kinds of paragraphs, such as descriptive, reason, how-to paragraphs and more.

Example: The Descriptive Paragraph

Sam is my cool pet frog. First, he is small, bumpy, and green. His big round eyes look around in my room when he is awake. Also, he has long legs with black spots on them. They help him hop and jump in my tank.

During first writing drafts, it is important to maintain basic sentence structure and punctuation. If the student writes in run-on or fragmented sentences, it will be harder to make revisions later. Immediately after the sentence or sentences are written, the student needs to go back and look at spelling errors, and correct any punctuation and capitalization errors. The main goal is to develop writing fluency, the act of writing out complete thoughts.

Practitioners can try to model how to proofread by presenting a short, written piece that needs to be revised and checked for punctuation, capitalization, and spelling errors. There are many student writing books that offer such drill and practice opportunities.

100

At the same time, the student needs to refer back to his original list and make sure the outline was followed correctly.

Many dyslexic students will still write as little as possible. These hesitant writers must be pushed to use more and more detail.

An example of a "boring" paragraph:

Richard had five pets in his house. First, he had a dog named Lou. Also, he had a cat named Judy. Finally, he had three goldfish named Jeff, Nancy, and Stephanie. Richard enjoyed having all his pets.

Many students find this task very scary and must be encouraged to equate writing to painting a picture. Instead of using paints, magic markers, or crayons, they will be painting a picture with words!

When the student has mastered the basic paragraph, it is time to take the next step by creating expanded paragraphs. Expanded paragraphs add additional detail sentences to each supporting sentence in the basic paragraph.

An example of a more interesting paragraph with expanded elements:

Richard had five adorable pets in his house. First, he had a big, fluffy dog named Lou. She liked to play fetch and tug of war with her toy bone. Also, Richard had a Siamese cat named Judy. She liked to jump up on his lap and watch television. Finally, Richard had three bright, orange goldfish named Jeff, Nancy, and Stephanie. They would come rushing up to the top of the tank when Richard came over to feed them. Richard really enjoyed playing with and taking care of his pets.

THE BIG FIVE ESSAY/THE FIVE PARAGRAPH ESSAY

All standardized testing is now expecting students to write an essay with five basic paragraphs. It starts with the thesis/topic paragraph, continues with at least three supporting paragraphs, and ends with a concluding paragraph.

Students will follow the same strategies they utilized for writing the basic paragraph. Effort is still needed to create the organizing list and outline, and transitional/signal words are still helping to connect ideas together.

The basic organizational writing patterns must be remembered as well. However, with so many more details to be included, it becomes even more important to incorporate the descriptive vocabulary words that add nuance.

The outline or list for the essay now becomes more detailed. Once the topic is decided, then the student needs to decide how many sub topics will be needed to adequately discuss everything. Each sub topic is now a separate paragraph.

Example:

Essay Topic: Caring for Goldfish is Easy

1)	**The Tank**	**Topic Sentence**
	correct amount of water	supporting sentence
	gravel can be used	supporting sentence
	keep bottom clean	supporting sentence

2)	**The Water**	**Topic Sentence**
	change ¼ every week	supporting sentence
	replace all water if cloudy	supporting sentence
	no chemicals in the water	supporting sentence

3)	**The Food**	**Topic Sentence**
	flaked food	supporting sentence
	clean lettuce	supporting sentence
	don't overfeed	supporting sentence

It is important to note that the outline/list is never solid. In other words, the outline is forever changing as the writer continues to make decisions about the content of his composition. Students should remember that the outline/list is a tool for good organization. So, if an idea is not working, the writer will delete it from the outline. On the other hand, if the writer comes up with a new idea, it should be incorporated into the outline.

Many students gain more confidence when they can see a very clear beginning, middle, and ending to their writing assignment.

The Thesis Paragraph now replaces the Topic Sentence. It often begins with a general statement. Then it focuses the point of view or opinion. It ends with the thesis statement.

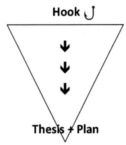

Each Supporting Paragraph should begin with a Topic Sentence. This will make it easier for the student to transition from one major point to the next major point. The same organizational goals are followed that were originally part of the basic paragraph.

The Concluding Paragraph needs to summarize the entire essay, while not becoming an exact copy of the Thesis Paragraph. Too often, students tire at the end of the writing assignment and rush to get it done by repeating the same information.

Evaluation of Writing

1. **Content** – Does the student effectively express ideas?
2. **Organization** – Can the student write in complete sentences and paragraphs?
3. **Structure** – Can the older student (upper elementary and above) use particular forms like comparison, cause and effect, etc.?
4. **Mechanics** – Can the student adequately punctuate, capitalize and spell? The delayed reader may be given exemptions on the spelling piece, or use of a spell check device for assistance.

Suggestions to Promote Independent Writing

1. **Written Conversations** – have students sitting by each other communicate only through writing
2. **Correspondence** – writing to relatives, friends, pen pals etc.
3. **Journals** – daily diary of events
4. **Memory Photo Album** – writing captions and or narratives about a family trip or vacation

These are formal writing assignments; therefore, sentence structure, punctuation, and spelling are always checked and proofread.

COMPREHENDING AND WRITING NARRATIVE TEXT (FICTION)

FOUR IMPORTANT ASPECTS OF COMPREHENSION

1. The purpose of reading is to understand, enjoy and learn from material. Students with reading delays often think reading means recognizing words.
2. Comprehension is an active process and accurate process. Good readers construct a text in their minds as they read.
3. Comprehension uses background material or schema. When students understand concepts important to a story, their comprehension increases.
4. Comprehension requires higher-level thinking skills. Good readers combine their own background information with the information in the text to draw conclusions.

During the reading process, it is crucial for the struggling student to be actively engaged in the reading. In order to develop and strengthen fluency, the student must be reading, from word to word, from line to line, from beginning to end of the passage. For some children, reading aloud is an important tool for them to use. Many will benefit from using their index finger or pencil to guide them. When a practitioner is working with the student, he or she must decide how often, or how quickly, to correct reading mistakes that the child makes. It is a balancing act between maintaining comprehension, while assisting in the fluency of the reading.

In narrative texts, stories are told and plots unfold. Narratives have characters and a plot with a sequence of events. Most are fiction, but some chronicle real life events.

Narratives are written to inspire personal responses. The reader becomes involved in narratives they read. The reader puts himself in the character's place.

However, studies show that poor reading comprehension is more common with readers who have poor language skills and who are more isolated from natural learning opportunities. These readers most often come from home environments where reading, writing, and access to the arts is limited. These readers have more difficulty thinking outside of the concrete world. They are often unable to use inference to relate the fiction they read with their own daily life.

Therefore, it is crucial for the practitioner to set up a bridge between the narrative text and the student before and during the reading process. This can be done in a variety of ways:

1. **Building background information**. Introduce new concepts and new vocabulary to the student.

   Example: Before reading a story about a ranch, introduce new terms like *mare* or *foal*. Read a short non-fiction article about life on a ranch.

2. **Use Predicting Strategies**. Activate thinking skills by asking the students what they think the title of the story means. Try introducing important story words.

   Example: "The Witch in the Second Grade." Words include *magic, spells*, and *disappearing*.

Once the student begins reading the story, the practitioner can help promote better comprehension. The most common technique for this is The Directed Reading-Thinking Activity (DR-TA)

With DR-TA, the story is broken up into sections. After a section is read, (either silently or aloud) the practitioner asks questions that promote higher thinking skills and check basic factual knowledge.

There are several drawbacks to asking questions. The questions can unintentionally give away too much information, allowing for guessing. The questions can be too frequent or take so long to answer that the reader becomes tired and loses focus.

INTEGRATING READING AND WRITING

Writing their thoughts about materials they are reading helps students organize the ideas presented in the text and increases their comprehension. Here are some writing strategies that improve reading comprehension.

1. **Post-It Strategy** - To check for comprehension during the reading of a short story or chapter in a novel, the practitioner may want to try the "Post-It" strategy. Whenever the student stops reading he can write a simple summary on a Post-It note of what has occurred in the passage. At the end of the entire reading selection, the accumulated Post-It sheets can be used as a review of content. Older students can also explain the "author's intent" on the Post-It summaries. For instance, the summary might remind the reader that the author introduced a new character into the story line.

2. **Story Maps and Pyramids** - Visual diagrams that show students the elements that all stories contain. The student can use these maps to identify characters, setting, conflict, and solution. Practitioners can introduce blank story maps before reading has begun and ask students to fill them in as they go. Some maps are big enough that the student can actually write complete sentences that can later be used as a formal summary.

3. **Problem Solution Identification** - A chart is used to identify the problems or conflicts that arise in the story, and the resulting solutions. The student should once again try to write in complete sentences.

4. **Rewritten Stories** - After the student has read a story or a chapter in a novel, it can be summarized in their own words. The student can also be allowed to retell the story from one character's point of view.

5. **Writing to One of the Main Characters** - After the student has read the story, he or she can write a letter or postcard to a character.

6. **Writing a News Article About the Characters and Plot** - The student can pretend to interview characters in the story for a local newspaper.

7. **Novel Reading Log** - The student summarizes each chapter and writes a personal reaction to the content in a notebook. Older students can also write their thoughts about the intentions of the novelist.

These summaries are always formal writing assignments. Therefore, sentence structure, punctuation, and spelling are always checked and proofread.

THE ORTON-GILLINGHAM CLASSROOM

Because every classroom is already language based, the opportunity for the classroom to be an OG classroom is present. The key is to enable the student to "see" how language develops, from consonants and vowels, all the way to the comprehension of fiction and non-fiction passages. The student needs to be able to "see" how written expression develops from the noun and verb in the sentence all the way to the writing of the research paper.

The classroom belongs to the students. Often, classroom walls are filled with pretty pictures, seasonal displays, and motivational posters. While these are nurturing, they are usually only decorative and provide no real learning opportunity. However, in the OG classroom, every wall and bulletin board should convey to the student how language develops. The classroom should be a completely interactive world of learning and language that pertains to the students in that learning environment. As students participate in classroom lessons or complete assignments independently, they are constantly exposed to the language they need to become more proficient readers, writers, and mathematicians.

Upon entering the classroom, the observer will notice how each wall and bulletin board presents the progression of language. The bulletin boards begin with the basic phoneme sounds and continue around the room, progressing to each higher level of language. Just how sophisticated the wording and presentation of the bulletin boards become depend on the age and grade level of the class and the relevance to the students' level of learning.

Each bulletin board is interactive and promotes multi-sensory learning.

The bulletin boards are learning centers that constantly help students utilize language in all content areas and also provide daily practice for the development of language for:

- phonemic awareness
- phonics instruction
- reading fluency
- spelling

- vocabulary
- comprehension of fiction
- comprehension of non-fiction
- grammar
- written expression

Each bulletin board can be changed with new examples of:

Concept	Board
Phonemes	#1 - "Letters are Talking"
Syllables	#2 - "Six Syllable Families"
Syllabication Rules	#3 - "Let's Divide"
Latin and Greek Roots	#4 - "Affixes Help You Understand"
Spelling Rules	#5 - "Follow the Rules"
Sentence Structure	#6 - "Sentences Need"
Paragraph structure	#7 - "Paragraphs Need"
Reading Comprehension	#8 - "Read to Learn"

The final board represents the culmination of the progression of language, with reading comprehension of narrative stories and novels, and reading comprehension of nonfiction expository articles and textbooks.

BULLETIN BOARD #1: LETTERS ARE TALKING!

In a primary classroom, the "Letters are Talking" board is used each day as a "tuning fork" for students to review the sound/symbol associations of previously introduced phonograms and the introduction of new phonograms.

The teacher can lead the class by reviewing the previously introduced phonograms on the board. As the teacher points to a phonogram, the students review the phonogram by saying the letter's name, key word, and sound, while tracing the shape on their desktops with the index finger of their writing hand.

Example: a, apple, /ă/

Once all the phonograms are reviewed, the teacher may choose to introduce a new phonogram. On the board or large card, the teacher should present the new phonogram by saying its name, introducing a keyword that begins with the phonogram sound, and making the sound.

Example: b, boy, /b/

The students will repeat the letter name, keyword, and sound while tracing the letter on their desktops with their writing hand. This daily drill fosters the multisensory aspects of learning by combining the visual letter, the auditory sound of the letter, and the physical shape of the letter.

Levels of "Letters are Talking" Boards

Emergent and early readers will have "Letters are Talking" bulletin boards that highlight the basic letters/sounds of the alphabet. This board can present single consonants that are dependable in sound: *b, d, f, h, j, k, l, m, n, p, r, s, t, v, x, y,* and *z*.

Then, the board could present consonant digraphs, which are two consonants that make one sound: *sh, ch, th, ph, ck*; and consonant blends, which are two or three consonants blended together. Beginning blends can include *st, gr, cl, sp, pl, tr, br, dr, bl, fr, pr, cr, sl, sw, gl,* and *str*. Ending blends can include *nd, nk, lk, rt, nk, lk, rt, nk, rm, rd, rn, mp, ft, ct,* and *pt*.

Also, long and short vowel sounds, like the short sound of vowel /ă/ as in *cat* and the long sound of vowel /ā/ like in *rate* could be introduced.

New phonograms are introduced only when the teacher is confident that the students have developed automaticity of previously learned phonograms.

By first and second grade, the "Letters are Talking" bulletin board can highlight more advanced phonogram combinations, such as vowel combinations (diphthongs), where two vowels make one sound. Also, there are the long vowel combinations including *ai, ay, ee, ea, oa, ow,* and *oe,* and the more unusual vowel combination sounds which include *ou, au, aw, oi, oy, oo, ew, ue* and *ui.*

In addition, other phonograms introduced could include r-controlled vowels, including: *ar, or, er, ir, ur, ear, war,* and *wor;* unusual consonants like *c* and *g,* which have two sounds; and irregular spellings that do not match traditional open and closed syllables. They include *all, alk, old, olt, oll, ost, olk, ild, ind,* and *igh.*

If the teacher does not have a thorough knowledge of phonics and phonetics, the introduction of phonemes selected may actually impede the students' developing reading fluency.

Generalizing phonogram sounds into actual reading opportunities is crucial for developing reading fluency, which is the ability to smoothly and accurately blend the phoneme sounds into syllables and words at an even pace. Therefore, the students must be reading daily in order to begin generalizing phonograms (sound / symbol) from drills to actual content. Too often, the students are not able to take their growing knowledge of phonograms into actual reading opportunities.

The teacher should be utilizing either phonetically-controlled readers or basal readers and content area texts, in order to have the students begin to recognize the phonograms as they read words. Of course, the reading materials selected should be at a reading level that matches the student's current knowledge and proficiency of previously introduced phonograms.

BULLETIN BOARD #2: SIX SYLLABLE FAMILIES

5 Syllables

open
| no | a |

closed
| not | at |

silent e
| note | ate |

double vowel
| ēe | ēa | āi | āy |
| meet | meat | rain | play |

r-control
| är | ör | ër | ïr | ür |
| star | fork | her | girl | burn |

Before this bulletin board is used, students need a thorough introduction to the syllable. They should know that a syllable has one vowel sound and that a syllable is produced by one pulse of breath.

The six syllable types should be introduced one at a time, when the students are ready to be introduced to the new concept.

- **Closed Syllables** end with a consonant. The consonant cuts off the sound of the vowel. Therefore, the vowel sound is short.

  Example: /ŏ/ as in *not*

- **Open Syllables** end with a vowel. The vowel is not cut off by a consonant. Therefore, the vowel sound is long (the vowel can say its own name).

  Example: /ō/ as in *no*

- **Silent e Syllables** end in a silent final e. The silent e at the end makes the vowel before it have a long sound (the vowel can say its own name).

  Example: /ō/ as in *note*

- **Diphthong /Vowel Team Syllables** usually have two vowels that have one sound ("w" can be used as a vowel). It is best to begin with two vowels that make a long sound: *ai, ay, ee, ea, oa, oe.* Then, introduce, when students are ready, the irregular double vowel sounds: *ou, au, aw, oo, ue, ew, ui, oi, oy,* etc.

- **R-controlled Syllables** have at least one vowel followed by an r. The most basic r-combinations are *ar, or, er, ir, ur* as in *star, fork, her, bird,* and *burn.*

- **The Consonant-le Syllable** ends in an unstressed vowel. This syllable type may be best introduced on the next board entitled, "Let's Divide Syllabication."

  Example: *apple*

To make the bulletin boards interactive, the words used as examples can be changed every day.

The Syllable Bulletin Board can be an aid for developing reading fluency and spelling in the content areas. As each syllable type is introduced, daily practice and drill opportunities should be provided to help students recognize the syllables when reading, writing, and spelling. One strategy utilizes current content area materials. For example, after a page is read from a social studies chapter, the students can look for and identify the syllable types on the page if needed. Eventually, students will be looking for all six syllable types as they read. This will enhance fluency (reading smoothness) and spelling. This same strategy can be used when the student is reading a fictional passage.

The students can refer back to the bulletin board when trying to reference a syllable type during drill exercises, reading opportunities, and writing assignments. Many vocabulary workbooks and many phonics workbooks may have a few pages designated to introduce the syllable types. These lists or exercises can be used for more practice opportunities.

BULLETIN BOARD #3: LET'S DIVIDE!

LET'S DIVIDE!

| Compound | Words | bath/robe | side/walk |
| | | sail/boat | home/sick |

Root/Suffix

Twins

VC/CV

Vowel Y

Consonant **le**

V/CV

VC/V

As the students are learning and reviewing the six syllable types, the next step is to string these single syllables and words together. The resulting words are multisyllabic. Not all of these syllables are complete words, so they must join with other syllables.

The ability to smoothly read multisyllabic words lies in knowing where one syllable ends and the next one begins. This is made more possible when students can recognize the six syllable types within these words and know the vowel sound each one makes. This is the key to fluency.

The Orton-Gillingham Classroom and the visual bulletin boards can help the students understand how letters become syllables and syllables become words. The students can look at the three bulletin boards: "Letters are Talking," "The Six Syllables Families," and "Let's Divide!" Students can "see" the progression of language and how individual phonograms form syllables and how syllables form words.

Different Ways to Divide a Word into Syllables:

Compound Words

The first type of multisyllabic word is the compound word, made up of two smaller words joined together. Different compound words can be placed on the board each day. These could be chosen to help students review syllable types or introduce vocabulary from the content areas for science, social studies, and math. This is a good time to integrate the six syllable types with the new concept of multisyllabic words. On the board, on reading lists, in reading passages, etc., the student can divide the compound words while saying it aloud.

Root Word/Suffix

The second type of multisyllabic word is the root/suffix, which is made up of a root word and a suffix ending. Adding the suffix allows the writer to describe actions. This means that root words may be changed when joining the suffix. Different root/suffix words can be placed on the board each day. These can be chosen to help students review syllable types or introduce vocabulary from the content areas of science, social studies, and math. Since most of the suffix endings are closed syllables, root words should be taken from all six syllable types.

118

THE VC/CV Pattern and the "Twins"

When two consonants stand between two vowels, the syllables are divided between the consonants. If the consonants being divided are the same, they are often called "Twins." These words are called "Rabbit" words.

Vowel Y

When the letter *y* is used as a vowel, it will usually be seen at the end of the word. In a one syllable word, the vowel *y* borrows its sound from long vowel /ī/ as in *shy, cry,* or *my*. In a multisyllabic word, the vowel *y* will often borrow its sound from long vowel /ē/ as in *sunny, carry, ugly,* or *chewy*.

With the knowledge of the vowel *y*, students can use three ways to divide a multisyllabic word. For example, with the word **sunny**. The *y* "borrows" its sound from long vowel /ē/ and "befriends" the next consonant, so it has company in the syllable. Also, this two-syllable word can be divided by saying that there are twins to be separated. Finally, use the spelling pattern of VC/CV and divide between the two consonants.

Consonant-le

It is also an important way to help students divide multisyllabic words. The consonant-le syllable is the final syllable in a multisyllabic word. It is a hard syllable to remember because the final e is silent. Many students have trouble pronouncing this syllable and spelling it. For example, *jungle* can be spelled *jungul*. The trick, or strategy, is to remind the student that this multisyllabic word has a final syllable with three letters: a *consonant+l+e*. Also, the students can look for twins when dividing some of these words, such as **bottle** or **puzzle**.

THE VCV Spelling Pattern

Understanding this syllable type may be the most important way for a student to understand how a multisyllabic word can be pronounced. When a student mispronounces a word, it usually happens because the wrong vowel sound is being used. This means that the reader is dividing the syllables apart at the wrong spot. For example, if the reader uses a short vowel sound, when a long vowel sound is the correct choice, the word will not make sense (with a word that is already in their vocabulary). If the reader uses a long vowel sound, when a short vowel sound is the correct choice, again, the word will not make sense.

As this bulletin board is utilized, the multisyllabic words should be changed daily. They can include words from content areas including literature, social studies, science, and math. As the rules of syllabication are introduced, the teacher can provide daily practice to help students recognize the rules when reading, writing, and spelling. Students can use current content area reading passages to generalize the syllabication rules from drill to actual practice.

BULLETIN BOARD #4: AFFIXES HELP YOU UNDERSTAND!

Affixes
help you understand
new words

Prefixes

un = not	**unhappy**
in = not	**inexpensive**
re = again	**remind**
ex = out	**extend**
pro = forward	**propel**

Suffixes

ness = having	**unhappiness**
ly = how to	**inexpensively**
ful = full of	**remindful**
able = can be	**extendable**
er = that which	**propeller**

Roots

pens = weigh	**inexpensively**
tend = to stretch	**extendable**
pel = to push	**propeller**

As the students continue to practice integrating the six syllable types into multisyllabic words, it is time to introduce the concept of Latin and Greek roots and parts of speech. Now, the student is moving from simple reading fluency to the development of reading comprehension. Grammar is the set of rules that describe how to structure language. To become proficient readers and writers, students must understand the structure of grammar. It is crucial that grammar be a daily and consistent part of all curriculum. As the student reads content or writes about concepts learned, grammar connects all thoughts together.

The "Affixes Help You to Understand" board will display a growing list of basic prefixes, roots, and suffixes that can aid in the knowledge of new vocabulary. Students learn that word parts do not stand alone. They come to realize that affixes and roots carry information that can help them understand the meaning of new words. This is crucial in the comprehension of content area curriculum: social studies, science, math, and literature. On the Bulletin Board, the listed affixes can be presented in a color code: prefixes – green; roots – blue; suffixes – red; or like a traffic light: prefixes – yellow (caution, there might be a spelling or pronunciation change); roots – green (everything is good to go since roots are often phonetic); suffixes – red (stop because there is often a schwa and there is sometimes a spelling change when adding a suffix).

For younger students in elementary school, it is best to present the suffixes -ed, -s, and -ing, followed by open and closed syllable prefixes first. These types of prefixes are usually the most common, so the students can use their knowledge of the syllable types to quickly learn how the meaning of a word can change.

The Affixes Board will also include suffixes.

Depending on the age and grade level of the students, suffixes help to teach the concepts of tense, agreement in number, and the descriptive use of adjectives and adverbs.

- tie: *un*tie, *re*tie, *un*ties, *re*ties
- pack: *un*pack, *re*pack, *un*pack*ed*, *re*pack*ing*

The students learn that suffixes can change the meaning of a word. The daily study and review of grammar can provide students with the structure of language they need to be able to comprehend text and write their thoughts into words.

The Orton-Gillingham Classroom Bulletin Boards can help students see the progression of language and how words can become different parts of speech, which will affect the content of the sentence. For elementary grade students, the introduction of each Latin root is best done when it plays a part in the understanding of curriculum content. For example, in a social studies class, if the students are learning about moving goods from one country to another country, then it would be a good opportunity to introduce the root *port* (to carry). With their knowledge of the prefixes *ex-* (out) and *im-* (into), they can have a deeper understanding of *export* (to carry or send out) and *import* (to carry or bring in) as they are reading.

The "Affixes Help you to Understand" bulletin board can highlight content area vocabulary words as they are introduced. Therefore, the board will be constantly introducing and reviewing vocabulary as the students learn new content curriculum.

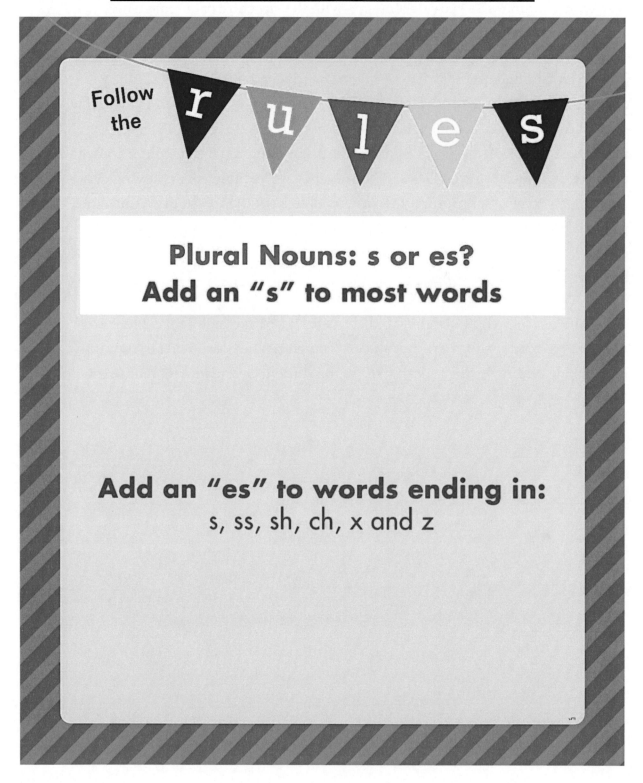

Follow the
r u l e s

Plural Nouns: s or es?
Add an "s" to most words

Add an "es" to words ending in:
s, ss, sh, ch, x and z

Knowing the spelling rules can assist students in reading fluency, comprehension, writing, and spelling. Becoming proficient in spelling means that the students have gained a connection between the sound/symbol associations of the phonograms, the six syllable types, and the rules of syllabication.

A reason why the spelling rules are vital to reading fluency can be seen in these simple examples:

hop ⇨ hopping
hope ⇨ hoping
grip ⇨ gripping
gripe ⇨ griping

Students begin to realize how knowing the six syllable types, the syllabication rules, and the spelling rules can help them more quickly recognize words when reading. Just as the students need to know the grammar rules to understand the structure of language, they must also learn about the spelling patterns and come to see that these rules are consistent most of the time.

Spelling rules are presented at the time that they can assist students in reading fluency and written expression. The spelling rules also assist the students as they encounter new vocabulary in the content areas. Most language books for younger students will have words with plural endings. This means that the spelling patterns are helping the students to see how suffixes can change form. This knowledge can assist students in reading fluency. Whenever a new rule is presented, examples of the rule should be included.

Here are several spelling rules to use this Bulletin Board with younger students:

Plural Nouns: *-s* or *-es*?
Plural nouns are words that mean more than one.

- Add an *-s* to most words.

    Examples: cat – cat*s*; shirt – shirt*s*; book – book*s*

- Add **-es** to nouns ending in *s, ss, sh, ch, x,* and *z.*

Examples: brush – brush*es;* watch – watch*es;* box – box*es*

The F.L.S. (Floss) Rule – also called the FLSZ
One syllable words ending in *f, l, s,* or *z* directly after a single, short vowel, usually end in double *ff, ll, ss,* or *zz.*

Examples: stu*ff,* be*ll,* cla*ss,* fi*zz*

Remind the students that these syllables are closed and have a short vowel sound. The students should also be made aware that there are exceptions to each rule. It is not necessary to have the students memorize the exceptions but to learn them when necessary. Students can be introduced to the F.L.S. (Floss, FLSZ) Rule when they have become proficient in the short vowel sounds. To help students generalize this rule from drill to practice, the teacher can photocopy a page from one of the readers and have the students look and circle the words that follow this rule.

The Doubling (111 and a Vowel) Rule
When a one-syllable word, with one vowel, ends in one final consonant, or the one-syllable base word ends in *CVC,* double the final consonant before adding a suffix that begins with a vowel.

(111) + (V)
Example: big + er = bigger

Drop the Silent e Rule:
If a word ends with a silent e, drop the e before adding a suffix that begins with a vowel.

Examples: hop*e* + ing = hoping; brav*e* + est = bravest

If a word ends with a silent e, keep the e when adding a suffix that begins with a consonant.

Example: hop*e* + ful = hop*e*ful; brav*e* + ly = brav*e*ly

The teacher can remind the students that the Silent-e syllable keeps the long vowel sound when the suffix is added. Also, the teacher can remind students of how the suffix ending can change the meaning of the word and the part of speech.

The Vowel Y Rule
If a word ends in the vowel *y* when a consonant precedes it, change the y to i and add the suffix.

> Examples: cry + s = cries; fry + ed = fried (do not change y to i before suffixes that begin with *i*; flying.)

If the vowel *y* is "married" to another vowel, then the vowel *y* must stay y.

> Examples: play + ed = played; toy + s = toys

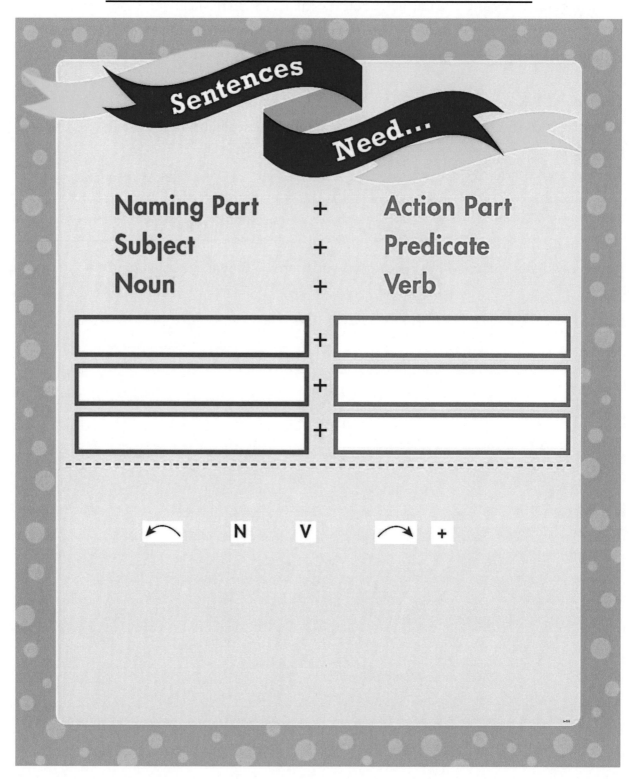

The "Sentences Need" bulletin board should present new sentences each day. This will allow the students to see examples of how sentences can vary. They can practice labeling sentences for *subject, predicate, nouns, adjectives, verbs, adverbs,* and *prepositions.* In fact, students can be asked to write sentences for inclusion on the board.

The "Sentences Need" board can also present the different types of sentences: *declarative, interrogative, imperative,* and *exclamatory.* The board is also a useful way to review punctuation and capitalization.

In reading and writing sentences, the students should first be aware of:

> Naming Part + Action Part
> Noun + Verb
> Subject + Predicate

New sentence examples should be placed on the board every day. The students will be reminded of the concepts previously introduced. As new elements are learned, they will be added to the current sentences displayed. The teacher can use pages from grammar books and have the students practice labeling the parts of speech that they recognize. The act of writing sentences and labeling parts of speech is multisensory: the student is physically interacting with text.

Paragraphs Need...

Topic Sentence
(main idea)

Signal Words
(help you write)

Signal Words

GO Words

Second

Next

STOP Words

Finally

Last of all

In conclusion

The students should be reading and writing sentences and paragraphs daily.

Students must learn that the topic sentence is the main idea of the paragraph. When they write a paragraph, they should always begin with the topic sentence. The supporting sentences should match what the topic sentence is introducing. Students should be taught that transitional words or signal words join the supporting facts together. Transitional words are sometimes called "signal words."

These words give the students directions about what facts are coming up next as they read. They help students follow the writer's thinking. In addition, the students learn that signal words also assist them when they are writing as they connect ideas together.

The "Paragraphs Need" bulletin board should present new examples each day. In fact, students can be asked to write paragraphs for inclusion on the board. The "Paragraphs Need" bulletin board can also present different types of paragraphs: *sequence, time order, cause / effect, comparison/contrast, reason, example,* and *description*. The topic sentences and signal words can be highlighted by color coding the words.

Fiction

Not real
A made-up story

Dangerous Storm

Genre:
Adventure

**Comprehension
Strategies**

Story Map

Questions to Answer

Nonfiction

Real
Facts about real things

Tornadoes

Genre:
Article

**Comprehension
Strategies**

Outlining

Note-taking

This board allows the students to compare different types of content. *Fiction and nonfiction should be taught in different ways.*

Fiction is narrative text. Students should be shown strategies for understanding setting, character, and plot.

Nonfiction is expository text. Students should be shown strategies for recognizing paragraph patterns, along with topic sentences, transitional words, and supporting facts.

The board will compare topics that can pertain to both nonfiction and fiction passages. Reading selections should be taken from the content curriculum in science, social studies, mathematics, and literacy. New examples are placed on the board as they are introduced from the content areas.

The "Read to Learn" Bulletin Board is the culmination of all the components of the Language Continuum. The Orton-Gillingham classroom will enable the student to become more aware of language; in fluency, comprehension, and written expression.

ADDITIONAL RESOURCES

(Visit us on the web at www.Whizzimo.com/Educator
for downloadable versions of some of the following resources.)

WORDLISTS

VC WORDS

in	it	on	am	at	an
if	up	us	Al	ad	id
oz	ox	ow	ax	Ed	

CVC WORDS A-Z

A	had	can	man	tax	bad	sat	gas
B	but	job	big	box	bad	bed	web
C	can	cut	cup	cat	cap	con	mac
D	had	did	red	led	bad	bed	mid
E	get	men	set	yet	let	red	yes
F	fig	fit	fat	fun	fed	fox	fix
G	get	got	fig	big	gas	gap	leg
H	had	him	hot	hit	hat	hip	hut
I	him	did	fig	six	big	mit	bit
J	job	jim	jet	jam	jug	jig	jog
K	kid	kit	ken	kin	kip	yak	wok
L	let	led	lot	leg	lit	lab	lip
M	him	man	men	yum	mit	met	mid
N	not	can	man	men	run	ten	sun
O	not	got	job	top	box	lot	hot
P	top	map	cup	gap	tip	pan	cap
Q	quit	quiz	quid	quin	quip	quite	quiet
R	run	red	ran	rev	rat	rod	rep
S	set	six	yes	sun	sat	gas	sit
T	not	but	get	set	yet	let	got
U	but	run	yum	cut	sun	sum	cup
V	van	rev	vat	vet	vox	vim	vex
W	web	win	wet	wit	wax	wed	wig

X	six	tax	box	mix	fox	fix	wax
Y	yet	yes	yum	yen	yin	yon	yam
Z	zen	zip	zed	fez	biz	zap	

DIGRAPHS

INITIAL DIGRAPHS

CH	chap	chin	chip	chat	chad	chop	chum
CI	social	special	financial	species	sufficient	official	
PH	phone	phase	physical	emphasis	telephone	phrase	photo
SH	shim	ship	shot	shop	shut	shed	sham
TH[1]	thin	thud	method	three	think	month	kind
TH[2]	that	this	than	them	then	thus	the
TI	quotient	potential	patient	nutritious	inferential	palatial	seditious
WH	when	whip	whim	whit	whiz	wham	whap

1 – unvoiced 2- voiced

ENDING DIGRAPHS

CH	such	much	rich	coach	each	speech	touch
CK	back	lack	rock	jack	neck	pick	sick
DGE	edge	knowledge	judge	bridge	ridge	lodge	dodge
PH	graph	triumph	Ralph	digraph	Joseph	paragraph	lymph
SH	wish	fish	cash	rush	dish	mesh	rash
TCH	match	catch	dutch	switch	pitch	stretch	sketch
TH	with	path	bath	math	south	lath	health

INITIAL AND ENDING DIGRAPHS

which	check	thick	shock	Chuck	shack	thatch
thrush	thrash	chock	shuck	thresh	church	sheath

136

CONSONANT BLENDS

TWO-LETTER INITIAL BLENDS

BL	black	block	bless	bliss	bluff	blush	blot
BR	brush	brick	brass	bred	brad	broth	brill
CL	class	clan	click	club	clock	cloth	cliff
CR	cross	crop	crack	crash	crush	crab	crib
DR	drop	dress	drag	drum	drill	drip	drab
DW	dwell	dwarf	dwindling	Dwight	dwindle		
FL	flat	flesh	flag	flash	fled	flap	flip
FR	frizz	fresh	frog	fret	frock	froth	frill
GL	glass	glad	glen	gloss	glut	glib	glum
GR	grass	grid	grip	grab	gram	grin	grim
PL	plan	plus	plot	plug	plum	pluck	plush
PR	process	press	present	problem	provide	practice	private
SC	scan	scab	scud	scat	scoff	scull	scuff
SK	skin	skill	skull	skip	skim	skid	skiff
SL	slip	slid	slot	slim	slab	slack	slit
SM	small	smith	smell	smash	smack	smug	smog
SN	snuck	snap	snack	snug	sniff	snuff	snag
SP	spot	spin	span	spell	spun	spill	spit
ST	still	step	staff	stop	stock	stuff	stick
SW	swiss	swim	swell	swam	swish	swig	swum
TR	track	trip	truck	trap	trick	trim	trash
TW	twin	twig	twill	twenty	twice	twist	twelve

THREE-LETTER INITIAL BLENDS

CHL	chloride	chlorine	Chloe	chloroform	chlorophyll	chlorinate
CHR	christ	chronic	chromosome	chloride	chronicle	chronicles
PHL	pamphlet	phlegm	phlebitis			
PHR	phrase	phrases	pamphlet	pamphlets	phrasing	phrased
SCH	school	strong	described	street	scram	unstrap

SHR	shrimp	shrub	shrink	shrug	shrill	shriek
SPH	sphere	sphinx	stratosphere	biosphere	sprint	sprawl
SPL	split	spleen	splash	splice	splendid	splurge
SPR	spring	spread	spray	sprinkle		
SQU	square	squeeze	squad	squirrel	squat	squid
STR	strong	scram	stress	string	struck	strict
THR	three	threat	threatened	threshold	threats	thread

TWO- AND THREE-LETTER ENDING BLENDS

CT	fact	act	effect	project	object	direct	product
FT	left	soft	shift	gift	draft	lift	craft
LD	old	help	self	child	told	held	felt
MP	camp	jump	pump	lamp	prompt	stamp	damp
MPT	attempt	prompt	contempt	exempt	tempt	unkempt	
NCH	French	branch	inch	lunch	bench	ranch	bunch
ND	and	end	hand	find	mind	land	kind
NT	went	sent	plant	spent	grant	print	rent
PT	kept	script	swept	slept	apt	crept	wept
SK	risk	ask	task	desk	mask	dusk	flask
SP	grasp	crisp	asp	prism	gasp	spasm	clasp
ST	most	just	must	last	best	next	past

INITIAL AND ENDING BLENDS

plant	stand	trust	spent	print	trand	blind	blimpadraft
brand	tract	craft	swept	slept	blond	crisp	plump

138

SYLLABLE TYPES

CLOSED SYLLABLES

3 Sounds	with	not	but	had	which	can	when
4 Sounds	just	hand	help	went	film	click	soft
5 Sounds	French	scram	glitch	bring	length	plant	stand
6 Sounds	strong	spring	string	strict	script	prompt	strand

OPEN SYLLABLES

1 Open Syllable	be	he	we	she	no	so	me
2 Open Syllables	data	micro	china	ago	via	zero	hero

MAGIC E SYLLABLES

A-E	made	same	state	make	case	take	came
E-E	theme	Steve	swede	grebe	Pete	Eve	
I-E	time	like	life	while	line	white	side
O-E	home	role	note	close	close	code	hope
U-E (cute)	muse	mule	cute	fuse	mute	puke	fume
U-E (June)	rule	june	tube	duke	crude	tune	rude

R-CONTROLLED SYLLABLES

AR	part	far	hard	start	tarp	parts	march
ER	her	per	terms	term	verb	hers	clerk
IR	first	third	girl	sir	firm	birth	girls
OR	for	form	york	short	north	forms	nor
UR	church	turn	turns	hurt	burst	fur	burn
WAR	war	warm	warning	wars	award	ward	reward

139

WOR	work	world	words	word	working	works	workers
ARR	carry	marry	barrel	carrot	parry	arrow	narrow
ERR	Jerry	Terry	ferry	berry	cherry	merry	errand
IRR	mirror	irritant	irrigation	irrational	irritate		
ORR	sorry	correct	worry	horror	borrow	corrupt	torrent
URR	current	hurry	curry	flurry	turret	furry	scurry

VOWEL TEAM SYLLABLES

AI - r(ai)n	main	pain	faith	claim	daily
AI - cert(ai)n	certain	captain	portrait	curtain	bargain
AU - (au)tumn	cause	August	audience	fault	author
AU - (au)thority	Augustus	restaurant	trauma		
AW - s(aw)	law	draw	raw	awful	straw
AY - pl(ay)	may	way	day	say	away
EA - st(ea)k	great	break			
EA - (ea)t	each	mean	least	reason	east
EA - br(ea)d	head	death	read	meant	heavy
EE - f(ee)t	see	between	three	need	keep
EI - v(ei)n	reign	vein	veil	beige	feign
EI - c(ei)ling	either	receive	protein	seize	weird
EI - for(ei)gn	forfeit				
EIGH - sl(eigh)	weight	eight	freight		
EU - sl(eu)th	neutral	peudo	neutron	deuce	Zeus
EI - f(eu)d	eulogy	feudal	Euclid	eureka	euphoric
EW - gr(ew)	new	knew	shrew	drew	crew
EW - f(ew)	nephew	skew	curfew	spew	phew
EY - th(ey)	suvey	grey	hey	prey	obey
EY - k(ey)	money	valley	journey	attorney	turkey
IA - potent(ia)l	initial	essential	Egyptian	partial	influential
IE - p(ie)ce	studies	field	believe	series	chief
IE - p(ie)	die	tried	lie	modified	implies
IGH - n(igh)t	right	high	light	fight	bright

IO - profess(io)nal	question	action	function	production	situation
IOU - relig(iou)s	audacious	obnoxious	fictitious	egregious	cautious
OA - b(oa)t	approach	road	load	loan	throat
OE - t(oe)	goes	Joe	echoed	foe	heroes
OI - c(oi)n	point	voice	choice	avoid	oil
OO - st(oo)l	too	school	room	food	soon
OO - b(oo)k	good	look	took	stood	wood
OU - s(ou)p	you	group	youth	coupon	acoustics
OU - s(ou)l	shoulder	poultry	mould	boulder	
OU - tr(ou)t	about	out	found	south	amount
OU - d(ou)ble	country	young	previous	touch	nervous
OW - sn(ow)	own	know	low	grow	below
OW - c(ow)	how	now	power	allow	flower
OY - b(oy)	employ	joy	destroy	loyal	Roy
UE - bl(ue)	due	issue	virtue	pursue	Sue
UE - h(ue)	value	argue	tissue	fuel	Tuesday
UI - s(ui)t	fruit	juice	recruit	cruise	bruise
	buy	Guyana			

CONSONANT-LE SYLLABLES

LE	little	table	able	single	middle	simple	sample
LES	samples	tables	titles	angles	struggles	battles	temples
CKLE & KLE	ankle	tackle	sprinkle	sickle	trickle	buckle	chuckle
STLE	castle	whistle	bustle	rustle	thistle	nestle	hustle

Syllable Division Types

COMPOUND WORDS	upon	itself	within	onset	something
PREFIXES & SUFFIXES	prevent	illogical	displace	government	being
VC/CCV	children	control	country	include	approach
V/V	real	science	create	client	fluid
V/CV	about	over	even	data	human
VC/CV	also	only	after	system	under
VCC/CV	transfer	kingdom	empty	childhood	symptom
VC/V	any	given	very	never	power

ORGANIZATION OF A STUDENT BINDER

Put tabs with the following: *This is filed on top so the student's latest copy is on top. The number of tabs in the student's notebook depends what you are working on and how many tabs you want to have.*

1. Alphabet – if they are younger
2. Syllables – C L O V E R
3. Dictation
4. Learned Words - Spelling
5. Syllable Division
6. Oral Reading

Sample of a Younger Student's Binder with Tabs:

- Alphabet/Sequencing
- Syllables – Activities for the six syllable types
- Dictations
- Learned Words
- Reading

Sample of an Older Student's Binder with Tabs:

- Syllables – Activities for the six syllable types
- Dictations
- Learned Words
- Reading
- Affixes (Prefixes / Suffixes)
- Syllable Division

DEVELOPMENTAL TASKS FOR PHONOLOGICAL AWARENESS

Segmentation	Task
Sentences	Can you say a sentence and clap each time you say a word? *My cat is big*.
Compound Words	Can you clap one time for each little word? *backpack*
Syllables	Can you clap for each part of the word? *Atlanta*
Phonemes	Can you say each sound in the word? *Mop /m/ /o/ /p/*
Rhyming	Task
Discrimination	Do mat and cat rhyme? *Map and mop*?
Production	Tell me a word that rhymes with *bit.*
Isolation	Task
Initial	Tell me the first sound in the word *tent*.
Final	Tell me the last sound in *truck.*
Medial	Tell me the middle sound in the word *mat.*
Deletion	Task
Compounds/Syllables	Say *blackboard.* Now say it again without the *black.*
Phonemes	Say *tan.* Now say it again but don't say the /t/ an.
Substitution	Task
Initial	Say *pat*. Change the */p/ to /h/ hat*.
Final	Say *man.* Change the */n/ to /t/ mat.*
Medial	Say *look.* Change /oo/ to /i/ lick
Blending	Task
Compounds/syllables	I'll say the parts of the words and you will guess what the word is: bun ny
Phonemes	I'll say the sounds of a word and you will guess what the word is: /r/ /i/ /g/ /f/ /a/ /t/

SAMPLE ORTON-GILLINGHAM LESSON PLAN #1

VISUAL DRILL: Today's Letters _____

_____

Practitioner shows the card. Student says the name, keyword, and sound while tracing the letter form.	List any student errors:	Explain your error correction.

AUDITORY DRILL: Today's Letters _____

_____

Practitioner hides the card while saying the sound. Student says the name of the letter while tracing or writing the letter.	List any student errors:	Explain your error correction.

BLENDING DRILL: (Rapid Exchange)

Practitioner uses the card deck to build a word. Student says the word.	List any student errors:	Explain your error correction.

NEW SIGHT WORDS: Today's New Words

_____

_____

Practitioner shows and says the word. Student repeats the word. Practitioner says letter names and student repeats. Student writes the word three times while saying the letter names. Student closes his eyes and traces out the word while saying the letter names.	Review the words that were the most difficult for the student.

SIGHT WORD REVIEW: Today's Words_____

_____

Practitioner shows the word. The student says the word, spells out the word, and says the word again.	Review the words that were the most difficult for the student.

REVIEW WORDS TO READ: Today's Words_____

_____

Practitioner prepares sheet with review words. Student reads each word	List any student errors.	Explain your error correction.

INTRODUCTION OF NEW CONCEPT: New Phonogram - Practitioner will model writing the new letter while providing keyword and sound. New Spelling Rule – Practitioner will model how the rule is done.

NEW CONCEPT:_____

NEW WORDS TO READ: Today's Words_____

_____

Practitioner prepares sheet with new words. Student reads each word while tracing or tapping out the letters.	List any student errors.	Explain your error correction.

SPELLING SOS

NEW WORDS TO SPELL: Today's Words _____

_____

Practitioner says word. Student repeats the word, says the sounds, and writes out the word while saying each sound. Student reads the word after writing it.	List any student errors.	Explain your error correction.

REVIEW WORDS TO SPELL: Today's Words _____

_____

Practitioner says word. Student repeats the word, says the sounds, and writes out the word while saying each sound. Student reads the word after writing it.	List any student errors.	Explain your error correction

DICTATION SENTENCES: Today's Sentences _____

_____

Practitioner says the sentence two times. The student repeats the sentence back. The student writes the sentence while saying each word.	List any student errors.	Explain your error correction.

READING: Student reads the passage orally while using the index finger or a card for tracking. The reading selection may be made up of phrases, sentences and / or whole passages. The reading selection may or may not be phonetically controlled, depending on the needs of the student. Practitioner should correct misread words and have student read the word or sentence again.

SUMMARY OF LESSON AND PRESCRIPTIVE DECISIONS FOR NEXT LESSON

_____

_____

_____

SAMPLE ORTON-GILLINGHAM LESSON PLAN #2

Name: _____ Date: _____ Lesson #:_____

I. DRILL

__1. Show/say (cards): 3- 5 minutes
__3. Dictate sounds: 3- 5 minutes
__5. Read back last dictation: 3- 5 minutes

Error Correction **(from last lesson's spelling and/or reading to be addressed in this lesson)** If in reading, include in your Jewel Box drill. If in spelling, include in dictation.

II. Extra practice: Jewel Box word cards (previously taught skills) **plus previously taught red words (written in red non-phonetic) Fluency building (about 25 words or less)**

III. Letter Formation – if necessary (Manuscript or cursive)

IV. Learned Words/Red words __Sight __High Frequency __Categories or __Everyday

V. NEW PHONOGRAM/CONCEPT or REVIEW: Direct instruction (VAKT)

___ New Concept Card __Trace letter (3x's) __Multisensory Instruction __Read Words

Materials:
Procedure:
Words to read that follow this new or review concept (If review different from those in Jewel Box):

VI. SPELLING DICTATION: words

1.	4.	7.	10.
2.	5.	8.	11.
3.	6.	9.	12

VII. SPELLING DICTATION: phrases

1.
2.

VIII. SPELLING DICTATION: sentences (Include red words taught in this lesson and those previously taught along with previously taught skills. Make sentences rich with review)

1.
2.
3.
4.
5.

**Read back spelling words, phrases, and sentences before going on in lesson

IX. Identifying Syllable Types or Syllable Division: (when appropriate and necessary)

1.	4.
2.	5.
3.	6.

X. ORAL READING: ____Phrases/Sentences ___Story ___Re-read for fluency ___Check comprehension ___Record errors

Reading Material Name: **Story –**

XI. Game: (when appropriate and necessary)

SAMPLE ORTON-GILLINGHAM LESSON PLAN #3

Teacher: _____ Lesson Plan #: ____

Student: _____ Date: _____

Warm-Up:

| |
| |

Drill: Visual and Auditory

Phonological Awareness/Syllable Activity:

| |
| |

Review and Reinforcement:

Words to Read:

Words to Spell:

Sentences to Read:

| |
| |

Sentences to Write:

| |
| |

Review Sight Word(s):

| |
| |

New Information: _____

Words to Read:

Words to Spell:

Sentences to Read:

| |
| |

Sentences to Write:

| |
| |

New Sight Word(s):

| |
| |

Oral Reading:

| |
| |

Practitioner Notes from the Lesson:

| |
| |

SAMPLE SCOPE AND SEQUENCE #1

a /ă/	all	ey /ē/
c	-tch	c /s/
d	wh	g /j/
g	th /th/ voiced	au
o /ŏ/	-nk (ank, ink, onk, unk)	aw
s	-ng (ang, ing, ong, ung)	ph
qu	open syllable	-dge
i /ĭ/	ay	ch /k/
b	ai	Doubling Rule
h	ee	ost
j	ea /ē/	ind
l	y /ē/	old
u /ŭ/	oa	ild
m	ow /ō/	olt
n	oe	wa
p	y /ī/	qua
r	igh	Silent-e Rule
t	silent-e syllable	silent letters (wr, kn, gh, gn, mb, mn)
y	oo /oo/	ar /er/
e /ĕ/	oo /oo/	or /er/
f	ar	-ed
k	or	-s
v	er	tion
w	r-controlled syllable	ture
x	ou /ow/	sion
z	ow /ou/	Y Rule
-ck	vowel team syllable	war
sh	eigh	wor
th /th/ unvoiced	oi	augh
initial consonant blends	oy	ough
flsz rule	ew	ie
final consonant blends	consonant-le syllable	ei
closed syllable	ir	eu
ch	ur	ue

SAMPLE SCOPE AND SEQUENCE #2

LEVEL 1	-all - ball	ph /f/	war as in ward
m	-ck rule - duck	-igh	**TEACH AS NEEDED**
/ă/	-tch rule - witch	r-controlled syllable	u as in push
t	-dge rule -badge	ar /ar/	-alk as in talk
s /s/	ch /ch/	or /or/	-alt as in salt
b	th- voiced	er /er/	-augh vs -ough
t	wh	1-1-1 doubling rule	ch /k/
f	sh	E dropping rule	ch /sh/
c /k/	Magic E syllable	-tion /shun/	wa as in water
i /ĭ/	ost, ind, old, ild, olt	-sion /shun/, /zhun/	qua as in squash
h	VC/CV division	ir /er/	-que vs -gue
n	Soft c /s/	ur /er/	x /gz/ as in exit
p	Soft g /j/	Y changing rule	-se /z/ nose
concept of a syllable	-ng	LEVEL 3	-se /s/ nonsense
Closed syllable	-nk	a /ə/ schwa	air - hair
d	VC/CCV – VCC/CV division	ey /ē/	oar - boar
f	LEVEL 2	ey /ā/	-oor moor
g	Open syllable	-ture	-eer pioneer
r	y/ē/	ie /ē/ middle of a word	-ear as in hear
n	y/ī/	ie /ī/ end of a word	-ear as in bear
o /ŏ/	V/CV division	ou as in mouse	-ear as in heard
g /g/	-s, -ing, -ly, -ful, ness, -ment	ou as in soup	-ear as in hearth
h	-less, -est	ou as in trouble	-our as in hour
j	-ed /ed/, /t/, /d/	au /au/	-our as in journey
l	s/z/	aw /au/	-our as in tour
p	VC/V division	ea / ĕ/	-our as in course
r	Consonant + le syllable	ea /ā/	wor as in word
u /ŭ	Consonant + le division	eigh /ā/	arr as in arrow
j	Vowel team syllable	ue as in true	err as in berry
w	ee	ue as in rescue	irr as in mirror
k	ay	ew as in few	orr as in borrow
e /ĕ/	oa	ew as in grew	gn /n/
y /y/	ai	or /er/ doctor	-mb /m/
v	ow /ō/	eu as in Europe	-mn /m/
w	ea /ē/	eu as in neutral	gh/g/ as in ghost
x /ks/	oe /ō/	ar /er/ dollar	-gh /f/ s in laugh
qu	oy /oi/	ui as in fruit	wr /r/ as in write
z	oi /oi/	Accenting rules	kn /n/ as in kneel
initial consonant blends	oo as in foot	2-1-1 doubling	i /ē/ as in patio
final consonant blends	oo as in food	V/V division	ou /ŭ/ as mother
flØss rule- ff, ll, ss, zz	ow /ou/	war as in homeward	

CHECK OFF LIST FOR THE AUDITORY DRILL

The following chart will enable a practitioner to quickly keep track of the phonograms used during the Auditory Drill.

Sound	Letter	Key Word(s)
Short /a/	a	apple
Long /a/	a, a-e, ai, ay eigh, ei, ey, ea	baby, ape, rain, play weigh, vein, hey, steak
/b/	/b/	bat
/k/	c, k, ck, ch,	cat, key, sock, school
/d/	d, ed	dog, sailed
Short /e/	e	egg
Long /e/	e, y, e-e, ea, ee ei, ie, ey	me, happy, eve, eat, feet, ceiling, piece, money

/f/	f, ph	fan, phone
/g/	g	gate
Short i	i	igloo
Long i	i, y, i-e, ild, ind, igh, ight	hi, cry, ice, wild, kind high, light
/j/	j, g	jet, gym
/l/	l	lock
/m/	m	mask
/n/	n	nest

Short /o/	o	octopus
Long /o/	o, o-e, oa, oe, ow	no, hope, boat, toe, row
/p/	p	pot
/kw/	qu	queen
/r/	r	rat
/s/	s, c	sun, city
/t/	ed	tent, jumped
Short /u/	u	umbrella

Long /u/	u, u-e, ue, ui ew eu oo	music, tune, blue, suit, flew, feud, food
/v/	v	van
/w/	w	web
/ks/	x	fox
/y/	y	yo-yo
/z/	z, s	zebra, nose
/th/ voiceless	th	thumb
/th/ voiced	th	then

/ch/	ch, tch	chair, match
/wh/	wh	whistle, whale
/sh/	sh	ship
/er/	er, ir, ur, ar, or	fern, fir, burn, dollar, doctor
/ed/	ed	rented
/oo/	oo	foot
/ou/	ou, ow	out, cow
/oi/	oi, oy	boil, boy
/au/	au, aw, augh ough	August, saw, taught, bought

LETTERS CHECKLIST

Letters	Basic level	Intermediate level	Advanced level
b	"b" bat		
c	"k" cat	"s" city	
ch		"ch" chin	"k" echo "sh" chef
-ck		"k" pack	
d	"d" dog		
-dge		"j" badge	
d(u)			"j" graduate
-ed	"ed' painted	"d" spilled "t'" jumped	
f	"f" fan		
g	"g" gum	"j" gentle	
ge		"j" fringe	
gh		"f" laugh	"g" ghost
gn			"n" gnat
gu			"g" guess
h	"h" hat		
j	"j" jam		
k	"k" kite		
kn			"n" know
l	"l" lamp		
-lf*			"f" calf
-lk*			"k" walk
m	"m" magnet		
-mb			"m" comb
--mn			"m" column
n	"n" net		
p	"p" pan		
ph			"f" phone
ps			"s" psychic
qu		"kw" quilt	
-que			"k" antique
r	"r" ring		
s	"s" sun		"z" rose
sc			"s" science

			"sk" scale
sh		"sh" ship	
t	"t"top		
-tch		"ch" catch	
th		"th" this "th" thin	
t(u)			"ch" picture
v	"v" vase		
w	"w" wagon		
wh		"hw" wheel	
wr			"r" write
x		"gz" exit "ks" box	
y	"y" yarn		
z	"z" zebra		

ORTON-GILLINGHAM CHECKLIST

This checklist is designed to assist the clinician in recording concepts that have been taught. Items are not presented in a particular order. Each item is introduced when appropriate.

CONSONANTS

ONE SOUND   **TWO SOUNDS**

b _____   n _____   c _____   _____

f _____   p _____   g _____   _____

h _____   r _____   x _____   _____

d _____   t _____   s _____   _____

j _____   v _____

k _____   y _____

l _____   z _____

m _____

CONSONANT DIGRAPHS

sh _____   th _____   _____

wh _____   ch _____   _____   _____

ph _____

qu _____

VOWELS

SHORT VOWEL SOUNDS   **VOWEL-CONSONANT-E**   **VOWEL R**

a _____   a-e _____   er _____

i _____   i-e _____   ir _____

o _____   o-e _____   ur _____

e _____   e-e _____   ar _____

u _____   u-e _____   _____   or _____

                              y-e _____

Vowel Teams - Diphthongs

ee_____   ea _____ _____   oi _____   oy _____
oa _____   ow _____ _____   ue _____   ew _____
oe _____   ie _____ _____   au _____   aw _____
ai _____   ey _____ _____   eu _____
ay _____   ei _____ _____
igh _____   oo_____ _____
                ou _____ _____ _____

Syllable Types

Closed _____   Open _____   Vce _____
Vowel Teams _____   R-controlled _____
Consonant–le _____

Spelling Rules

1. Floss _____
2. 1-1-1 _____
3. 2-1-1 _____
4. Drop the e _____
5. Regular Plurals _____
6. Plurals of nouns ending s, x, z, ch, sh _____
7. Plurals of nouns ending y _____
8. Plurals of nouns ending o _____
9. Plurals of nouns ending f, fe _____
10. Possessives: singular _____   plural _____
11. Plurals of letters, figures, signs _____
12. i before e _____
13. Suffix -ful _____
14. Suffix -ly _____

15. Vowel Y _____
16. Prefixes dis-, mis- _____
17. Chameleon prefixes _____

SPELLING GENERALIZATIONS

ch / tch _____   k / ck _____   ge / dge _____

OTHER PATTERNS

ing _____   ang _____   ink _____   all _____
ild _____   ind _____   old _____   olt _____
ost _____   oll _____
ed _____   _____   _____

SYLLABICATION RULES

1. A one-syllable word _____
2. A compound word _____
3. VC/CV _____
4. Root / Suffix _____
5. Prefix / Root _____
6. V/CV _____
7. VC/V _____
8. A vowel forms its own syllable _____
9. When two vowels come together and are sounded separately V/V _____
10. Consonant-le _____
11. al, el ending _____
12. ed ending _____

READING VOWEL CHART

a	a= baby = /ā/ a = apple = /ă/ a = Donald = /ə/ a = ball = /ô/	
ai	ai = rain = /ā/	
ay	ay = day = /ā/	
au	au = August = /ô/	
aw	aw = saw = /ô/	
a-e	a-e = cake = /ā/	
e	e= zero = /ē/ e = Eskimo = /ĕ/ e = Warren = /ə/	
ee	ee= bee = /ē/	
ea	ea= eat = /ē/ ea = bread = /ĕ/ ea = great = /ā/	
eigh	eigh = eight = /ā/	
ei	ei = ceiling = /ē/ ei = veil = /ā/	
ew	ew = grew= /ōō/ ew = few =/ yōō/	
ey	ey = key = /ē/ ey = they = /ā/	
e-e	e-e =these= /ē/	
eu	eu = Europe =/ yōō/ eu = neutral = /ōō/	
i	i = spider = /ī/ i = itchy = /ĭ/	

o	o = clover = /ō/ o = octopus =/ŏ/ o = Timothy = /ə/ o = compass = /ŭ/	
oa	oa = boat = /ō/	
oi	oi = coin = /oi/	
oy	oy = boy = /oi/	
ou	ou = mouse = /ou/ ou = soup = /ōō/ ou = trouble =/ ŭ/	
oe	oe= toe = /ō/	
ow	ow = snow = /ō/ ow = cow = /ou/	
oo	oo= food = /ōō/ oo = foot =/ŏŏ/	
o-e	o-e = bone =/ō/	
u	u = tuna = /ōō/ u = music =/ ū/ u = umbrella = /ŭ/ u = push =/ŏŏ/ u = Marcus = /ə/	
ui	ui = fruit = /ōō/	
ue	ue = true = /ōō/ ue = statue =/ ū/	
u-e	u-e = rule = /ōō/ u-e = cube = / ū/	
y	y= cry = /ī/ y = gym = /ĭ/ y = candy = /ē/ y = analysis = /ə/	
y-e	y-e = type = /ī/	

	i = Benjamin = /ə/	
ie	ie = thief = /ē/	
	ie = pie = /ī/	
i-e	i-e pine = /ī/	
igh	igh = light = /ī/	

READING CHART FOR CONSONANT LETTERS

Letters	Basic	Intermediate	Advanced
b	"b" bat		
c	"k" cat	"s" city	
ch		"ch" chin	"k" echo "sh" chef
-ck		"k" pack	
d	"d" dog		
-dge		"j" badge	
d(u)			"j" graduate
-ed	"ed' graded	"d" loved "t'" mixed	
f	"f" fish		
g	"g" gum	"j" gentle	
ge		"j" fringe	
gh		"f" laugh	"g" ghost
gn			"n" gnat
gu			"g" guess
h	"h" hat		
j	"j" jam		
k	"k" kite		
kn			"n" know
l	"l" lamp		
-lf*			"f" calf
-lk*			"k" walk
m	"m" mouse		
-mb			"m" comb
--mn			"m" column
n	"n" net		
p	"p" pan		
ph			"f" phone
ps			"s" psychic
qu		"kw" quilt	
-que			"k" antique
r	"r" ring		
s	"s" sun		"z" rose
sc			"s" science

			"sk" **sc**ale
sh		"sh" **sh**ut	
t	"t"**t**op		
-tch		"ch" ca**tch**	
th		"th" **th**is "th" **th**in	
t(u)			"ch" pic**tu**re
v	"v" **v**ase		
w	"w" **w**agon		
wh		"hw" **wh**eel	
wr			"r" **wr**ite
x		"gz" e**x**it "ks" bo**x**	
y	"y" **y**arn		
z	"z" **z**ebra		

RULE CHART

Short Vowel Rule	Plural Rules	Suffix Rules	Miscellaneous
FLØSS	ch, sh, s, x, z	1-1-1-doubling	c and g
-ck	o	e-dropping	ie/ei
-tch	f to v	y- changing	possessives
-dge	y	2-1-1 doubling	
	irregular		

SIX SYLLABLE TYPES CHART

C	vc (short vowel)	**Closed Syllable:** A closed syllable ususally has a SHORT VOWEL. *Never followed by an l, r, w, or y*	*Cat – stamp – path – stop*
L	c + le	**Consonant + le syllable**	*-ble, -fle, tle, -zle, dle, gle, etc*
O	v (long vowel)	**Open Syllable:**	*no – go – we – hi – she – me – he*
V	vv	**Vowel Team syllable**	*feet – snow – rain – moon – toe*
E	vce	**Magic E Syllable**	*make – like – bone – these – cube*
R	vr	**R controlled Syllable**	*car – bird – turn – her – fork*

SPELLING CATEGORIES

- u – as in put, push, pull
- Welded sounds –ang, -ing, ong, ung –ank, -ink, -onk, -unk
- Kind Old Words – wild, kind, old, most etc.
- –igh as in light
- –eigh as in eight
- –all as in tall
- –alk as in talk
- -alt as in salt
- –augh vs. –ough
- ch "k" Christ / ch "sh" chef
- wa as in water
- qua as in squash
- –que "k"antique / -gue "g" league
- Silent Letters kn- knight, wr-write, etc
- –se "s" nonsense /-se "z"nose
- –tion/-sion

SPELLING CHART #1

Short vowel spellings

"ă"	"ĕ"	"ĭ"	"ŏ"	"ŭ"

Long vowel Spellings

"ā" 8	"ē" 8	"ī" 6	"ō" 5	"yōō" 5	"ōō" 7

Consonants with multiple spellings

"d"	"f"	"g"	"j"	"k"	"m"	"n"	"r"	"s"	"t"	"z"	"ch"	"sh"

Vowel sounds with multiple spellings

"o͝o"	"ou"	"ô"	"oi"

Schwa Sound Spellings

"ə"	"ə"	"ə"	"ə"	"ə"	"ə"

SPELLING CHART #2

Short vowel spellings

"ă"		"ĕ"		"ĭ"		"ŏ"		"ŭ"	
a	apple	e	Ed	i	itchy	o	octopus	u	up
		ea	bread	y	cymbal			o	compass
								ou	double

Long vowel Spellings

"ā" 8		"ē" 8		"ī" 6		"ō" 5		"yōō" 5		"ōō" 7	
a	lady	e	zero	i	spider	o	clover	u	music	u	tuna
a-e	make	e-e	these	i-e	pine	o-e	bone	u-e	cube	u-e	rule
ai	paid	ea	eat	y	cry	oa	boat	ue	rescue	ue	true
ea	break	ee	bee	y-e	type	ow	low	ew	few	ew	grew
ei	veil	ei	receive	ie	pie	oe	toe	eu	Europe	oo	moon
eigh	eight	ie	field	igh	high					ou	soup
ay	pay	y	candy							ui	fruit
ey	they	ey	money								

Consonants with multiple spellings

"d"	"f"	"g"	"j"	"k"	"m"	"n"	"r"	"s"	"t"	"z"	"ch"	"sh"
d	f	g	j	c	m	n	r	s	t	z	ch	sh
-ed	ph	gu	g	k	-mb	gn	wr	c	-ed	s	-tch	ch
	-gh	gh	-ge	-ck	-mn	kn	rh	sc		-se	t(u)	
		-gue	-dge	ch				ps				
			d(u)	-que								

Vowel sounds with multiple spellings

"ŏŏ"		"ou"		"ô"		"oi"	
oo	book	ou	flour	a	ball	oi	boil
u	push	ow	cow	au	auto	oy	boy
				aw	saw		

Schwa Sound Spellings

a - Donald	e - Warren	i - Benjamin	o - Timothy	u - Marcus	y - analysis

172

VOWEL TEAMS

oa		boat	(long o /ō/
ai		paid	(long a /ā/)
ay		pay	(long a /ā/, at the end of the word)
ee		feet	(long e /ē/)
oe		toe	(long o /ō/ at the end of a word)
oi		oil	/oi/
oy		toy	/oi/ (used at the end of a word or syllable)
au		fault	/ô/
aw		law	/ô/ (at the end of the word or followed by l and n)
ui		fruit	/ōō/
ea	three sounds	eagle	/ē/ - bread /ĕ/ - steak /ā/
ey	two sounds	monkeys	/ē/ - they /ā/
ie	two sounds	thief	/ē/ - pie /ī/
oo	two sounds	food	/ōō/ - foot /ŏŏ/
ou	three sounds	mouse	/ou/ - soup / ōō/ - trouble/ŭ/
ow	two sounds	snow	/ō/ - cow /ou/
ei	two sounds	ceiling	/ē/ - veil /ā/
ue	two sounds	true	/ōō/ - rescue /ū/
ew	two sounds	grew	/ōō/ - few /ū/
ou	two sounds	feud	/ū/ - neutral /ōō/

WAYS TO DIVIDE WORDS INTO SYLLABLES

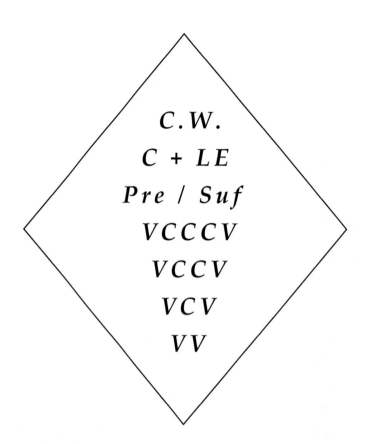

C.W.
C + LE
Pre / Suf
VCCCV
VCCV
VCV
VV

Teach young children in the following order:

VC/CV	rab/bit
VCCCV	os/trich
-cle	tur/tle
V/CV	ti/ger
VC/V	cam/el
V/V	li/on

Teach prefix and suffix division as you teach prefixes and suffixes

174

Orton-Gillingham Approach – Three Strands

Word Structure	Rules	Learned Words
- Letter sound/symbol relationships - Vowels - Blends/digraphs - Prefixes/roots/suffixes	- Spelling rules - Syllable types - Syllable division - Accenting	- High frequency words - Irregular spelling words - homonyms

MANNER OF ARTICULATION

Manner of articulation	Lips	Lips/teeth	Tongue between teeth	Tongue behind teeth	Roof of mouth	Back of mouth	Throat
Stop (unvoiced) (voiced)	/p/ /b/			/t/ /d/		/k/ /g/	
Nasal	/m/			/n/		/ng/	
Fricative (unvoiced) (voiced)		/f/ /v/	/th/ /th/	/s/ /z/	/sh/ /zh/		
Affricate (unvoiced) (voiced)					/ch/ /j/		
Glide (unvoiced) (voiced)					/y/	/wh/ /w/	/h/
Liquid				/l/	/r/		

ADDITIONAL HANDOUTS

(Visit us on the web at www.Whizzimo.com/Educator
for downloadable versions of some of the following handouts.)

Finger Spelling

if you are left-handed

1. Break the word apart by its phonemes (sounds), tapping the pad of each finger on the right-hand on a table (or in the air in front of a class) as each phoneme (sound) is segmented.
2. Then put the associated symbol for each sound on the same finger that had the sound. If one finger was represented for the sound, then only one finger is represented for the letter(s) by tapping the pad of the finger as above.

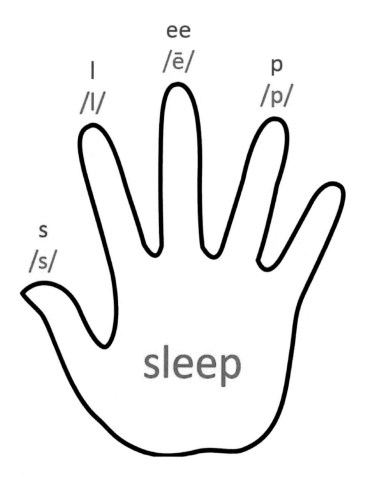

Use the <u>opposite hand</u> that <u>you write with,</u> so the pencil stays in the writing hand while the other hand can do the work (move each finger as you segment the sound).

Finger Spelling

if you are right-handed

1. Break the word apart by its phonemes (sounds), tapping the pad of each finger on the left-hand on a table (or in the air in front of a class) as each phoneme (sound) is segmented.

2. Then put the associated symbol for each sound on the same finger that had the sound. If one finger was represented for the sound, then only one finger is represented for the letter(s) by tapping the pad of the finger as above.

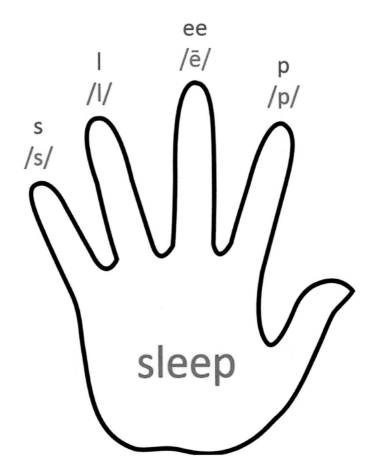

Use the <u>opposite hand</u> that <u>you write with</u>, so the pencil stays in the writing hand while the other hand can do the work (move each finger as you segment the sound).

"Gentle Cindy"

hhb '13

oh, y<u>ou</u> l<u>u</u>cky d<u>u</u>ck
(<u>ould</u>)

could   would   should

hhb · 11

Closed Syllable

- ends in a consonant
- the vowel is short

Silent-e Syllable

- ends in a silent e
- the vowel is long

Open Syllable

- ends in a vowel
- the vowel is long

r-Controlled Syllable

- has at least 1 vowel followed by r

Consonant-le Syllable

- always found at the end of a word
- to find this syllable, count back 3

Vowel Team Syllable

- has at least 2 vowels that make one sound

hhb '10

182

Closed Syllable

- ends in a consonant
- the vowel is short

căb/ĭn

Open Syllable

. ends in a vowel

. the vowel is long

hē/rō

r-Controlled Syllable

. has at least one vowel followed by r

. the vowel is neither long nor short

st<u>ar</u>

Vowel Team Syllable

- has at least two vowels together that make one sound

rain/bow

Silent-e Syllable

- ends in a silent e
- the vowel is long

plānė

Consonant-le Syllable

. this syllable is found at the end of a word

. to find this syllable, count back 3

tur/tle

1   2   3 ←

VC/CV Syllable Division

When two consonants come between two vowels, divide between the consonants; if more than 2 consonants come between the vowels, divide keeping blends and digraphs together.

răb / bĭt

v c   c v

VC/V Syllable Division

part 2

If the word doesn't make sense after dividing after the vowel, then your second choice is dividing after the consonant, which makes then vowel short.

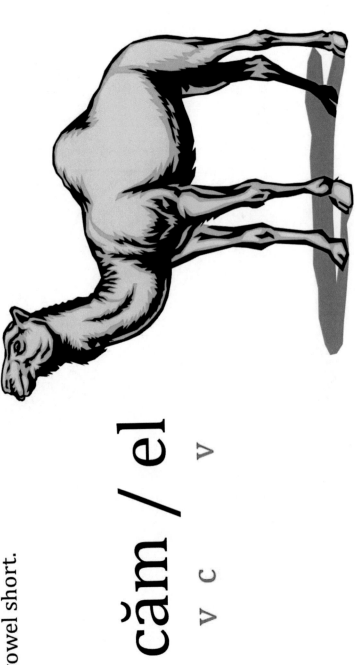

căm / el

v c   v

V/CV Syllable Division

part 1

When one consonant comes between two vowels, first divide after the vowel, which makes it long.

tī / ger

v   c v

V/V Syllable Division

When two vowels are together, divide between the two vowels, particularly if the two vowels do not form a vowel team; this will make the first vowel long.

lī / ŏn

Made in the USA
San Bernardino, CA
04 April 2019